Thomas Raleigh

Elementary Politics

Thomas Raleigh

Elementary Politics

ISBN/EAN: 9783337079253

Printed in Europe, USA, Canada, Australia, Japan

Cover: Foto ©Suzi / pixelio.de

More available books at **www.hansebooks.com**

ELEMENTARY POLITICS

BY

THOMAS RALEIGH

FELLOW OF ALL SOULS COLLEGE, OXFORD

SEVENTH EDITION

London

HENRY FROWDE

OXFORD UNIVERSITY PRESS WAREHOUSE
AMEN CORNER

1892

[*All rights reserved*]

Oxford
HORACE HART, PRINTER TO THE UNIVERSITY

PREFACE.

It has been truly said that if men would only define the terms which they use in argument, most controversies would end before they begin.

In the following pages I have attempted to define the terms which are commonly used in political argument. These terms are derived from history, from morals, from economic science, and from law. Some elementary knowledge of these sciences is necessary to the practical politician, just as an elementary knowledge of physical science is necessary to the mariner.

This book is not meant to be a compendium of information—nor is it meant to be a summary of orthodox political doctrine. My object is not to satisfy but to stimulate inquiry; not to form my reader's opinions, but to induce him to form opinions of his own.

Oxford, 1886.

PREFACE TO THE FIFTH EDITION.

In preparing this edition, I have corrected and supplemented some passages which were not sufficiently clear; and at the close of each chapter I have added references to those political and historical works which are most likely to be accessible and useful to the English reader.

Oxford, March, 1889.

CONTENTS.

			PAGE
CHAPTER	I.	THE ORIGIN OF SOCIETY	5
,,	II.	PRIMITIVE SOCIETY	9
,,	III.	CIVILISATION	15
,,	IV.	MODERN SOCIETY	22
,,	V.	THE MODERN STATE	34
,,	VI.	THE CONSTITUTION OF A STATE	43
,,	VII.	ELECTIONS	54
,,	VIII.	POLITICAL IDEALS	65
,,	IX.	PARTIES AND PARTY GOVERNMENT	78
,,	X.	WEALTH, ITS PRODUCTION AND EXCHANGE	90
,,	XI.	COMPETITION, MONOPOLY, RENT	98
,,	XII.	THE DISTRIBUTION OF WEALTH	108
,,	XIII.	SOCIAL INEQUALITIES	126
,,	XIV.	THE FUNCTIONS OF THE STATE	134
,,	XV.	THE STATE AND SOCIAL REFORM	151

CHAPTER I.

THE ORIGIN OF SOCIETY.

The first question we have to ask about society is the question how it was originally formed. Why do men live together in communities, and when did they first begin to do so?

Man is a very gregarious animal. He is easily affected by sympathy and the desire for sympathy. He prefers company to solitude. He admires and imitates others, and he likes to be admired and imitated.

Even if these social impulses were weaker than they are, man would be compelled by necessity to live a social life. No creature is more helpless, or less able to make a living, than a solitary man.

Seeing that society exists by nature and necessity, we are prepared to find that it has existed since men made their first appearance on this planet. Such is, in fact, the testimony of history. Here and there an individual or a family has subsisted apart from the rest of the human race. But the general rule is that men live, and always have lived, in social groups.

Theory of a Social Contract.

The foregoing account of society is directly at variance with a theory which has played a considerable part in European and American politics. In the 17th and 18th centuries, speculation on political subjects took a free course, and the teaching of history was not sufficiently regarded. Instead of piecing together such evidence as we have of the state of primitive man, ingenious writers sat down and proved, much to their own satisfaction, that society might or must have originated in a particular way. The chief result of their meditations was the theory of a Social Contract, which may be briefly stated thus :—

'In the beginning, men lived in solitude or in small family groups. Man was by nature good; his wants were few and easily supplied; he needed no government and feared no oppression. In course of time, men began to form larger groups. They then entered into a contract, whereby each was to receive the protection of all, and was in return to submit himself to the general will in matters of general importance. As soon as this contract was formed, selfish men began to take advantage of it to engross wealth and power to themselves. They also invented false doctrines in religion and politics to justify their encroachments. Such was the origin of luxury, poverty, kingcraft, priestcraft, and all the evils which afflict civilised humanity. And these abuses will never be redressed until we return to nature and restore to man the rights he possessed before society was formed.'

This theory looks very attractive, when it is set forth by a master of style like Rousseau; but it is contradicted at every point by facts. Man is not naturally good, any more than he is totally depraved. He is a being of mixed impulses, who requires discipline and education to make him definitely good. The supposed golden age, when men lived in peace and plenty, is a mere fiction,—the early history of mankind is a record of conflict and hardship. As for the Social Contract, there is not a scrap of evidence to show that any such transaction ever took place. Indeed, we know that it cannot have taken place as alleged; for the very notion of a binding agreement is strange to the mind of primitive man.

In spite of its unhistorical character, this theory has been widely received, especially among liberal politicians. People of a reforming turn of mind are pleased to be told that the abuses of which they complain are due to unjust laws, and that these laws are based on a mere convention which may be altered or annulled. Believers in popular government like to derive the authority of States from a compact to which all subjects were once parties; although, in point of fact, no government was ever founded on the free consent of all the people governed.

There is also something attractive in the use which this theory makes of the word 'nature.' Many men have regarded nature as a sort of deity, a 'power not ourselves which makes for righteousness'; an abstraction which makes no great demand on our faith, and yet a reality which we may reverence and obey. Transfer to 'Nature' the qualities of justice and goodness which belonged to God, and you have the creed of eighteenth-century liberalism. In like manner, 'human nature' is often appealed to, as if it were a high authority on moral and social questions.

It is well to remember that these phrases are not exact enough for careful reasoners. Strictly speaking, nature is only the aggregate of existing things and forces, some of which make for righteousness, and others not. Human nature is not the nature of men as they ought to be, but of men as they are; the term is wide enough to include all the impulses, good and bad, which make up the character of human beings in the mass.

The Social Contract theory is examined in Maine's *Ancient Law*, especially chap. ix, and in J. Morley's *Rousseau*. Many modern writers discuss the origin of society in terms of the doctrine of evolution; see, for example, Tylor's *Primitive Culture*. Herbert Spencer, in his *Principles of Sociology* and other works, treats society as an organism, of which individuals are the parts. In applying the idea of evolution to society, it is well to observe that there is a point in the development of man at which he becomes a self-conscious being, capable of summing up his own experience and of forming ideals which determine the course of his future evolution. When the individual members of society reach this point, society itself becomes consciously progressive.

CHAPTER II.

PRIMITIVE SOCIETY.

SOME thousands of years ago, society as it existed among our ancestors resembled in many points the societies which now exist among the more backward races of mankind. To understand the institutions under which we live, we must take note of the characteristic features of primitive life.

Customs.

Civilised society tries to guide itself by laws which are enforced because they are supposed to be just and convenient. Primitive society guides itself by customs which are enforced simply because they are customary. The origin of a custom may be referred to a divine being, or to some venerated ancestor, or to mere chance. But, once established, it is supposed to be established for ever. The 'law of the Medes and Persians which altereth not' was a customary law.

The force of custom is derived partly from tribal sentiment. All primitive communities regard their members as belonging to one family. The Jews, for instance, were all 'children of Israel,' though there must have been many among them who were not actually descended from Jacob. Every 'child of Abraham' was bound to observe the custom of his fathers.

In primitive times, religion and tribal sentiment are

closely identified. Any breach of custom is an offence against the tribal gods, and as such must be punished with rigour. This partly accounts for the severity of the ancient customary codes. 'The soul that sinneth, it shall die'; and every serious breach of custom was a sin.

The existence of a primitive people depends on their ability to form a body of customs strong enough to hold the community together, and to protect it against the attacks of its enemies and the self-will of its own members. When this difficulty has been overcome, the laws acquired by painful discipline are regarded in a spirit of religious conservatism. Primitive peoples do not admit the right of the individual to criticise the laws under which he is born. Even among civilised peoples, old customs survive and form the accepted basis of all law and politics. Most of our own laws are based on customs which prevailed ages ago among all the families of the Aryan stock to which we belong.

Though customs are supposed to be fixed, they change continually under the influence of new circumstances and new ideas. If you trace the early history of an institution—of marriage, for instance, or of property—you find that it is a history of development. During the period of custom, development is unconscious. During the period of law, you find conscious and unconscious processes of change going on at the same time.

Development of the Social Group.

Civilised society sets a high value on the rights of the individual man. In primitive times, a man as such had no rights at all. Men were divided into small groups, each of which was connected by a real or supposed community of blood. If an outsider came in and wished to join, he was at the mercy of the group: they might kill him or make him a slave, or they might adopt him, and so by a solemn fiction make him a full member of the community. Every person born or adopted into a clan was bound by its custom; if he broke the custom, justice would be meted out to him by the people or by the patriarchal chief who represented the authority of the real or mythical common ancestor. It is plain that no great advance in civilisation could have been made, unless the intense conservatism of this form of society had been broken up. It was in fact broken up among the Aryan races by a variety of causes.

As life becomes more settled, society naturally becomes local rather than tribal in its character. If a wandering clan settles down and forms a village community, the common name and blood gradually yield in importance to the common industry and household life. Wandering clans are always fighting, but village communities may live in peace together or even combine into a larger community. Some combination of this sort seems to have been the origin of the great city of Rome.

Again, as wealth and comfort increase, family life as distinct from social life begins to appear. It is no longer a daily necessity to combine with the whole clan; the individual has opportunities of considering himself and his children and of acquiring property apart from the common stock.

The power of the chiefs, whether elected captains or hereditary priests and rulers, tends to assist the breaking up of the clan. In peace, the chief provides for the cultivation of his land and the care of his cattle by bringing in outsiders to settle on the common territory. In war, he forms a band of picked men, who become an aristocracy, whether their hereditary position in the clan is good or not. If the chief extends his sway over many tribes he becomes a king: the sphere of government is widened, and national life begins to be possible.

Origin of Political Power.

In studying primitive society, we discover the origins of all the most important modern political institutions. Monarchy begins in submission to the captain in time of war, and in reverence for the chief who represented the common ancestor. Aristocracy grows out of the importance attached to blood, the respect due to the families most directly connected with the common ancestor. And we have seen how the chiefs, as their power developed, were able to form an aristocracy of personal service.

Nor is primitive society without its democratic features. In the assembly of the people, the chief presides; the elders and lesser chiefs speak; the people stand around to hear and approve what is done.

We must remember that primitive society knows nothing of the division of powers which is familiar to the modern mind. The chief is very often captain, judge, and priest. State, church, and family are one and the same body: and every member of the community does duty in the army, in the council, and in the common worship.

Origin of Property.

We may say that personal property has its origin in necessity. Moveable goods naturally belong to the person who has strength and skill to acquire them by conquest, industry, or barter.

But the wealth of primitive communities consists chiefly in land; and in land there was at first no individual property. Every member of a clan had a right to a maintenance out of the common land; and this right was protected by the custom of common cultivation and periodical redistribution. This arrangement has one qualified advantage. If a community is favourably situated on a fertile soil, the system of common rights produces a tolerably even social average of comfort; but wherever difficulties have to be overcome, the system fails, because it does not call out all the powers of the individual by throwing him on his own resources. Common cultivation and periodical redistribution are unfavourable to agricultural improvement, and therefore, in countries like our own, they gave way before a system of fixed rights of property in land. No doubt, in the course of the transition, the strong often helped themselves liberally at the expense of the weak. But the establishment of property in land was a great step towards the emancipation of industry from irrational customs and inferior methods of production.

People often speak in a sentimental tone of ancient society as if it had been more united and less selfish than modern society. But this is a mistake. Common rights in land, for example, were not maintained because people were enlightened and unselfish, but because they were so ill provided that no man could make a living apart from his clan or his village. And common rights were maintained by a balance of struggling interests, not without a good deal of quarreling and disturbance. There is, indeed, a strong social sentiment in primitive communities, but it is an unconscious kind of sentiment. Each man clings to his neighbours instinctively for help. In a civilised community each man has an opportunity of devoting himself consciously and considerately to the service of others.

For the place of custom in the history of civilisation, see Bagehot, *Physics and Politics*. The origins of property and the family are discussed in the works of Maine, who begins with the patriarchal stage of society; J. F. McLennan and others have carried the inquiry further back, to the barbarous customs of womancapture, etc., out of which the patriarchal household was developed. E. de Laveleye, in his *Primitive Forms of Property*, investigates the origin of property in land; the same subject is treated, from the English point of view, in W. Cunningham's *Growth of English Industry*.

CHAPTER III.

CIVILISATION.

PRIMITIVE society has produced many remarkable men, and has exhibited some fairly high types of industrial and political life. In Egypt, for instance, at a very early date there were many local communities, producing a large amount of wealth, gathered into one empire under powerful kings, and enjoying the ministrations of a learned priesthood. But with all these advantages, the state of Egyptian society was not satisfactory. The government was oppressive; the priests taught many false and absurd doctrines; the people were ignorant and improvident, and often in dire want. The wise men of Egypt never thought of attempting to remove these evils. They had never conceived the possibility of social progress. We may say, therefore, that in primitive society at its best the work of civilisation could hardly be said to have begun.

Greek Politics.

The Greeks learned their first lessons in art, in literature, and in science, from the Egyptians. But they introduced into all these departments of thought an element of their own. They were inquisitive, audacious, and clever beyond all other races; and they would be satisfied with nothing less than the free application of the human intellect to every subject of human interest. What they achieved in art and philosophy we need not now recount. But we must briefly consider what they achieved, and what they failed to achieve, in politics.

When the Greeks settled in Europe, they were divided into local communities, organised on the primitive model according to tribes and clans. In their history, and especially in the history of Athens, we can trace how the tribal gradually gave place to the local principle in government, and how the local community was developed into the City—a new political type, and a higher type than the world had yet seen. The Greek City was a true State, in the modern sense of the word, a body in which diplomacy, oratory, and administrative skill had full scope and opportunity. Society was passing out of the stage of unconscious development into a stage of conscious effort, directed to the realisation of liberty and equal laws.

Athens at the height of her fame may be regarded as the embodiment of all that was most advanced in Greek political ideas. But if we turn to the works of her historians and political thinkers, we find that they did not consider the Greek society of their time to be in a sound state. The philosophers were constantly returning to the question, What is virtue, and how may it be taught? And they looked on this question as one of immediate and even urgent importance to society. They felt that their countrymen were thinking too much of liberty, and far too little of discipline. And they foresaw that a people in this state of mind must fall before the power of some nation less cultured but better disciplined than themselves. The Macedonians, and after them the Romans, proved the truth of this forecast.

We can see now, even more clearly than the philosophers saw, the points where Greek society failed for want of a better moral standard. First, the Greeks were wanting in humanity. They made liberty the exclusive right of the superior people who were fit to be members of Greek states. Athens, for example, had only about 20,000 citizens, who obtained leisure for their public duties by turning over all the rough work to a much larger body of slaves. Even the wisest of them never dreamed that civilised life was possible without slavery. We are able to see now that slavery is, in truth, incompatible with civilisation. It is not enough that habits of discipline and courtesy should be formed in a limited class; social institutions are to be tested by the effects which they produce among men in the mass.

Again, the Greeks were sadly wanting in what we may call the submissive virtues—patience, self-denial, and the spirit of compromise and toleration. It was their self-will which embittered the faction fights in their cities between rich and poor, nobles and commons, friends of Athens and friends of Sparta. To gain a party victory all means were counted lawful—slander, treachery, and appeals to foreign powers for aid against political opponents. The vices of party spirit existed side by side with many fine moral qualities. In Greek society, human nature first had freedom to display itself, and it expanded vigorously towards the evil as well as the good.

Roman Law.

The Romans were not a brilliant people; they did but little original work in art and philosophy; but they possessed in full measure the practical virtues in which the Greeks were deficient. They were patient and methodical, fond of accounts and records, skilful in arranging compromises and in devising legal forms. The Greeks pursued their ideal of 'liberty and equal laws,' and forgot authority and discipline. The Romans held fast to authority, in the family and in the State; but they were very ready to concede rights to all kinds of subject persons. They allowed their slaves, their children, and their wives to acquire certain rights of property. And when they came to deal with foreign States and peoples, they admitted them also to a kind of equality by extending the right of Roman citizenship to their allies and subjects with an ever-increasing liberality. Subjection to Athens meant paying tribute and subserving the policy of a disdainful superior. Subjection to Rome meant participation in the benefit and glory of citizenship in the most powerful city in the world. This imperial policy was partly due to thoughtful self-interest, partly also to higher motives. With the instinct of a governing race, the Romans studied the institutions of the people over whom their influence extended; and they found a common element of equity and convenience pervading them all. This 'law of nations,' as they called it, was a great conception which contributed to widen the notions of lawyers and statesmen. When the Romans began to learn Greek philosophy, they acquired the notion of a 'law of nature,' wider in its scope than even the law of nations. This was the standard to which the wisest of them endeavoured to conform themselves and the laws which they administered: and they followed their ideal without forgetting the old Roman spirit of discipline. While they were reducing one country after another to subjection and order, they were also developing their law on rational principles, abolishing useless restraints, and making new rules suited to the requirements of a business community.

But the Romans, like the Greeks, failed to solve the problem, how the average man may be taught virtue. The 'law of nature' appealed to those who had a turn for self-culture and wise conduct, but it did not prevent ordinary people from being corrupt, unscrupulous, or cruel. Roman society in the time of Augustus was full of gross vices and superstitions, and there were those who thought that vice was prevailing over virtue, and that civilisation had been bought too dear. Better, said the satirists, better the early days of the Republic, when poverty kept wickedness within narrower limits.

Christianity.

The Christian Church was in its origin a society of people united by their faith in Christ, their hope of His coming, and their love for Him and for one another. It was a purely voluntary society, and at first it had no political significance. There is nothing in the New Testament to show that Christians as such were expected to redress social wrongs, or to produce a new type of civilisation. They stood aloof from the evil that was in the world; they looked forward to the time when Christ was to come triumphing over evil and subduing the world to Himself. Until Christ should come, His people were told to be patient, and to submit to the constituted authorities.

When the rulers of this world were converted, Churches of a different kind arose—powerful corporations, protected by and co-operating with the established governments. The primitive notion, that Christians were in the world but not of it, was not given up, but it was somewhat obscured by the fact that Christianity became a tribal, national, political religion, imposed by law on the subjects of every Christian State.

The theology and morality of the Bible, as interpreted by the Churches, entered into combination with the social forces which were at work in the Roman Empire. They did much to purify the old tribal customs; and when national governments began to be formed, they supplied a valuable element of order and union. They gave a new aspect to the Empire itself; the Holy Roman Empire, personified in the Pope and the Emperor, was a symbol of the unity of Christian civilisation. And wherever the missionaries of the faith formed a settlement, they carried with them a certain measure of learning, industry, and art.

The Catholic Church made one very important contribution to political thought by placing authority on a theological basis. Churchmen have always taught that man is a fallible and self-willed creature, who requires both law and gospel to put him in the right way. Properly stated, this doctrine is true to the facts of human nature; but the theologians exaggerated and distorted it. They were not content with asserting that man is sinful; they taught that every natural impulse is depraved (that is, turned away from what is good), and that man can become good only by thwarting his affections, and by denying what his reason prompts him to believe. Again, they were not content with showing that authority is a necessary element in education and government. They taught implicit obedience to the existing authorities in Church and State, and they took too little account of the fact that authority was vested in men as fallible and self-willed as the rest of mankind. They taught that Popes and Kings held a divine commission which it was sinful to oppose or even to criticise.

Mediæval Christianity produced noble types of character, and it showed, as Greek philosophy had never shown, how the social problem of the ancient world might be solved. But as a general rule its teachers did not consistently regard society from the moral point of view. They were hard on others, and not strict enough with themselves: they thought more of orthodoxy than of truth, more of piety than of virtue. They called themselves the shepherds of the people, but the people were scattered abroad as sheep having no shepherd.

For the subjects touched on in this chapter, I may refer to the histories of Greece and Rome; E. A. Freeman's *Comparative Politics*; and Lecky's *History of European Morals*.

CHAPTER IV.

MODERN SOCIETY.

It is not possible, nor desirable, to draw an exact line between ancient and modern history. No generation of men can take a fresh start; each generation must start with the habits and beliefs transmitted to it by its predecessors.

We may say that modern society had its origin in two movements which came to a head in the 16th century—the revival of science and scholarship which we call the Renaissance, and the revival of primitive Christianity which we call the Reformation. These two movements were intimately connected. The new learning would not have produced much effect on European society if it had not been combined with the enthusiasm of Protestant religion. And the Reformers could not have done their work without the scholarship which enabled them to destroy the very foundations of Papal and scholastic authority. But though science and religion worked together, they also worked separately, and even to some extent antagonistically. It is not easy to give in a short space any notion of a long historical process; but I must try to touch a few salient points.

Protestantism.

The Reformers asserted that the standard of truth and right was not the word of God as interpreted by authority and tradition, but the word of God as interpreted by the judgment and conscience of the individual believer. To this the partizans of authority replied, that if every man was to be his own interpreter, discipline would become impossible. They pointed out that Protestants differed hopelessly among themselves, and that some of the new sects were using the Bible to justify dangerous eccentricities of doctrine and conduct. In order to meet this reproach, Protestant leaders were compelled to construct a new system of authority in Church and State. They set in the forefront of their teaching the old Catholic dogma of the total depravity of man; they clung to the principle of coercion; and they had no doubt about their own ability to apply the law of God directly to social affairs. Of course Protestants were in a minority in Europe, and earnest Biblical politicians were in a minority even in Protestant countries. They were therefore reduced, like all minorities, to argue in favour of toleration and liberty of conscience; and their arguments were not without effect on themselves. But wherever they were in power, they thought that their duty to God required them to put down Popery; and when the Protestant Churches were once established, they refused to permit individual freedom of thought. This intolerance was not altogether indefensible. A movement like the Reformation produces a great variety of new opinions, and this variety may lead to hopeless confusion in practical matters, unless some measure of discipline is maintained by force.

Allowing for all drawbacks, the Reformation must be regarded as a considerable advance in the path of civilisation. In the first place, it was a protest against the corruptions of Catholic society, and it helped in many ways to purify the morals of Christendom. Again, it was a protest against excessive centralisation : it multiplied new centres of spiritual life. And though the Protestant principle of private judgment sometimes assumed irrational forms, it was in itself a useful principle, inasmuch as it required men to think for themselves, and to give up the notion that they could be saved by belonging to a certain religious corporation.

Secular Politics.

In the 16th and 17th centuries, all political questions were more or less connected with religion ; but it was precisely during this period that the secular notion of politics developed itself in the minds of thinkers and statesmen. In the works of Machiavelli (1469-1527) we find no trace of a religious or moral purpose. He treats politics as an intellectual kind of business carried on for the profit of the persons engaged in it; and this was the spirit in which the most accomplished politicians of that period usually acted. They dealt with religion itself in a Machiavellian way—not ignoring it, but using it as an engine of statecraft. This secularising tendency may be observed in the two powers which had most to do with the guidance of the Reformation in England and elsewhere.

First, we observe it in the rising power of royalty. When Papal authority was set aside, and feudal rights were giving way, it was natural that each nation should cling to the central institution in which its political life was embodied. Our own Tudor sovereigns proved the advantage to be derived by able princes from the changes that were taking place in theological and political opinion. Kings are usually compelled to regard religion from a secular point of view. Queen Elizabeth, for instance, did not shape her policy according to her religion (which was, as far as one can make out, a kind of Catholic sentiment), but according to the necessities of her position as chief of the Protestant interest.

Again, there was a secularising tendency in the middle classes, who made great advances in wealth and power during this period. The new form of evangelical religion laid hold of the merchants and gentry to a considerable extent; the new ideas flowed most steadily in the channels made for them by trade; the middle classes supported the royal power against the surviving pretensions of the Pope and the old nobility. They used their growing influence in a business-like way, discouraging exalted notions, and upholding safe practical compromises. In England they were strong enough to check the royal power itself, when the Stuarts attempted to revive the old type of authority in an Anglo-Catholic form.

It was from the secular side that toleration first made its way into politics. No religious body as such could quite approve of allowing all opinions to be taught with equal freedom. But religious individuals found they could combine for political ends without being at one on other questions of high importance. Thus, in Oliver Cromwell's army there were men of all sorts of odd opinions who did their duty equally well; and so throughout the whole army there came to be a feeling in favour of 'freedom for tender consciences.' And Cromwell himself, when he came into power, showed that it was possible to combine religious zeal with the worldly wisdom which recognises the impossibility of forcing everybody to be of one mind.

Humanitarianism.

During the 17th century, Protestantism made good its right to set up the Bible against the authority of the Church. During the 18th, the Bible itself was neglected or discredited by many able thinkers. There was an appeal to reason and humane sentiment against authority generally. There arose a school of writers who denied the dogma of human depravity both in its Catholic and in its Protestant form. 'Man,' they said, 'is naturally good; what he wants to make him perfect is not the guidance of authority, but liberty to follow his own instincts.' They traced all the evils of society to bad institutions, and to the false beliefs of persons engaged in the work of government and education. And they invited civilised mankind to return to nature, to abolish or reform their institutions, and to accept new laws, conceived in a spirit of respect for human rights and human goodness.

These theorists, of whom Rousseau (1712–1774) was the most eloquent, did good by exposing the barbarous absurdity of some laws which priests and statesmen thought essential to the well-being of society. Mere authority cannot produce social order, because it does not make people orderly by developing and relying on their better nature. But the unqualified assertion that 'man is naturally good' was a baneful falsehood, which has worked immense political evil. There is in each man a better nature which requires liberty for its development. But there is also in each man a lower nature—a stupid, greedy, short-sighted nature, which it takes a long struggle to conquer. Rousseau led people to think that there need be no struggle; that everything could be set right by changes in the social machinery.

The hopes of the humanitarians went sadly to wreck in the first French Revolution. French politicians began the 'return to nature' by destroying institutions, and for a time they were able to account for every failure by pleading that they had not yet destroyed quite enough. But after they had beheaded the King, and banished the nobles, and disendowed the Church, and massacred their enemies and one another, they only succeeded in making it plain that they had undertaken far more than they could perform. Their unfinished work passed into the hands of Napoleon, who had a kind of belief in the humanitarian formula, but never allowed that or any other formula to interfere with business.

The belief in the goodness and the easy perfectibility of man is still a powerful factor in liberal and democratic opinion. Until we attain to a sound view of human nature, democracy cannot be expected to make satisfactory progress. Politicians who wish to flatter us are still arguing, like Robespierre, that though laws may be unjust, though governing classes may be selfish, 'the people is never wrong.' But when we are asked to 'place unlimited confidence in the people' we must remember that *we* are the people—we who know well that we are no better than we ought to be. A wise man does not trust himself any further than he can see himself—and that is not very far.

Modern Industry.

Among those who applied the 'laws of nature' to society, the economists occupied a leading place. The doctrine of authority had been rigorously applied to the industry and trade of the civilised world. Governments thought it their duty to 'encourage industry' by giving bounties, levying duties, and maintaining a whole system of privilege, protection, and restraint. This policy was utterly condemned by Adam Smith (1723-1790) and his disciples. 'Men,' said they, 'engage in industry and trade for their own profit, and their own instincts will teach them what is profitable. Governments must learn to let people alone. If restraint and protection are removed, profitable industry will receive its full reward, and unprofitable industry will be crushed by competition. Let us have free trade between buyer and seller, between employer and employed, and nature will do the rest.' These opinions have never been consistently carried out by any Government; but in England since 1846 we have kept tolerably close to the lines of policy laid down by the economists. The results which we have obtained by doing so are of a mixed nature: so much the briefest summary of our recent history will disclose.

First, there has been a great movement of *expansion*. Enterprise and invention have been stimulated, and wealth has been produced on a scale which a hundred years ago would have been deemed impossible. A large proportion of the wealth produced has been saved and invested; our power of production increases continually with the increase of capital.

Again, there has been a movement of *diffusion*, owing to the freedom of combination permitted by modern law. Every man who has saved money has now an opportunity of investing it so as to obtain a share of the profits of undertakings carried on by Companies and managed by our ablest men. This diffusion of capital has greatly improved the position of the whole middle class, and of the labouring people who have money in banks and co-operative societies.

While there has been this tendency to diffusion there has also been a marked tendency to *concentration*, both of land and capital. Unrestricted trade offers great opportunities to the able and the fortunate. The possession of wealth gives a man every advantage in competing for more wealth, if he wishes to obtain it. A rich man can offer better terms to those who deal with him than a comparatively poor man. For all these reasons, industrial freedom favours the accumulation of great fortunes.

It is also to be observed that while our wealth has been increasing our wants have also increased. Expanding industry has offered employment to many hands, and has thus stimulated population. The rapid changes of modern trade are constantly throwing traders out of business, and labourers out of work.

And we must not forget that a wealthy society secures a chance of existence for multitudes who would simply be starved out in a poor, primitive community. Our small industries and our charities keep alive a host of people—weakly, or thriftless, or ill-behaved, or very unfortunate; and these form a kind of slough, into which the poorer labouring people are always in danger of falling. So our wealth increases, but the poor are still with us.

We perceive, then, that the results of free industry and commerce are very good and at the same time very disappointing. Economic freedom alone will not bring about all the good which the economists expected. They committed, as it seems to me, the mistake of arguing in this way: 'The hope of profit is man's natural guide in business matters; therefore we should leave it free and follow wherever it leads.' Just because it is natural, self-interest ought always to be held in check by caution, moderation, and unselfishness. Without this check, it must work mischief, even in business matters. In one man it takes the form of active acquisition, and he accumulates far more wealth than he can use. In another, it takes an indolent form; as soon as he has made a little gain, he marries and makes himself comfortable without thinking of the future. Now every one of the millions of men who constitute a civilised community is more or less led astray by self-interest, of the active or of the indolent kind. We need not therefore have much difficulty in accounting for our social troubles.

The Advance of Democracy.

During the last century, the principles of democracy have made great advances all over the world. In Europe, almost every nation has now a constitution, which professes to provide means for giving effect to the popular will. In America, the success of the United States has incited the Spanish colonies to declare themselves independent republics. Our own colonies have followed us, some of them think they have outstripped us, in developing free institutions.

The advance of democracy has brought with it a great improvement in the customs of civilised men. Our methods of government have become milder and fairer; the selfishness of ruling families has been checked; and laws are now made with due consideration for interests which were formerly ignored. Opinions are freely brought to the test of discussion, and tribunals have been created before which all parties may at least count on being heard. If you take the Statute-book and follow the course of English legislation since 1832, you will perceive how great and how salutary are the changes which have been wrought in every department of our social life by the extension of political rights.

At the same time, the candid historian of democracy has to record a good many failures and disappointments. It has been proved that corruption may flourish in republican soil, and that universal suffrage may pronounce an unjust and foolish judgment. The eighteenth-century philosophers, to whom democracy owes its creed, took but little account of the possibility of such failures. To them 'the people' was a kind of embodiment of nature and of the 'natural goodness' of man. Persons in authority were liable to prejudice and might make mistakes, but it was supposed that the unsophisticated judgment of common men must always be right. We have now had sufficient experience to know that this supposition is not true. Democracy has done good by bringing forward the subject multitude and giving them a right to speak; but it has not introduced us to any body of men whose judgment may always and in all cases be accepted without misgiving.

Progress.

I have endeavoured to touch, superficially but not carelessly, some critical points in the process by which primitive tribal communities have been developed into modern political communities. The process has been one of *evolution*, the higher type of society superseding and extinguishing the lower. Tribal conservatism has given way before industrial improvement and military discipline; religion has been gradually purified; the thoughts of the average civilised man are constantly becoming wider and clearer.

The movement of human progress is hard to follow: often we seem to lose sight of it altogether. It is not like the march of a regiment along the highway; it is like the advance of a crowd, making for some point which only a few know how to find. Look at them from a height and you see that each individual in the crowd has a path of his own. One keeps straight on; another is fetching a circle which will bring him back to his starting-point in due time; another has turned into the wrong road, and is calling the rest to follow him. Even those who hold the steadiest course are often turned back or aside by unexpected obstacles.

We cannot therefore undertake to map out the path of progress, either retrospectively or prospectively, with perfect certainty. We find the right path only by making a series of blunders, whether we plod along the track of our fathers, or dash into new ways of our own.

The student who wishes to understand the Reformation and its bearing on English politics should read Brewer's *Reign of Henry VIII*, Gardiner's *History*, Carlyle's *Cromwell*, and J. B. Mozley's articles on Strafford and Cromwell in his *Historical Essays*. The origins of toleration are well described in Masson's *Life of Milton*.

The humanitarian 'Gospel according to J. J. Rousseau' may be found in his works; see, for example, his *Discourse on the Origin of Inequality*. For the influence of his doctrine on the men of the Revolutionary period, see J. Morley's *Rousseau* and *Burke*.

CHAPTER V.

THE MODERN STATE.

WE have seen how the State arose out of the combination of tribal communities into cities and kingdoms. We are now to examine the modern State analytically, that we may know of what parts it ought to consist and what functions it ought to perform.

In a civilised country, the force of the community is vested in certain persons, for the purpose of defence and government. When the community acts by means of these persons it is called the State, and the members of the community are called subjects of the State. Laws are general rules made by the State for its subjects. Rights are claims recognised, and, if necessary, enforced by the State. In framing laws and defining rights the State should be guided by reason and justice; but its most characteristic and necessary attribute is force. Unless the laws and rights which it recognises can be made good against all opposition, the State ceases to be the State, and anarchy supervenes.

Observe that a civilised State derives its force from its own subjects. Without their manifold co-operation the Government would lose its political character, and would become like a hostile army encamped in the country. We sometimes say that a Government is strong because it has plenty of soldiers and police. It is more true to say that a Government is strong in proportion to the number of persons who believe in it; for each loyal subject helps to bring pressure to bear on those who may be inclined to disregard the law.

In order to exercise force on a great scale the State

must have wealth, and this also it derives from its subjects. In return for the protection it confers, property and persons within its jurisdiction are required to pay tribute. There is no bargain or competition in the case; the tribute is levied by force. Inasmuch as the State is exempt from competition, it is (not always, but generally) the most expensive of social agencies.

Before considering the parts of which a modern State is composed, we must take account of three principles which have been applied and combined in many different ways in forming political constitutions—the principles of monarchy, aristocracy, and democracy.

Monarchy.

The principle of monarchy is, that discipline is best secured by causing all orders to be issued in the name of a single person. Men whose minds are set on a common object usually place themselves under the command of a chief—the ablest, or the most plausible, or the highest in rank among them. For some purposes it is well to choose the ablest man to be chief; but there is often a distinct advantage in having a chief, whether he is an able man or not.

There are many types of monarchy. Three of these types seem to require separate consideration.

1. *Despotic monarchy.* The despotic king or emperor generally assumes that his power comes to him from God. He is therefore free from all human limitations, he is responsible to God only, and not to his subjects. Some despots have taken a high view of their duties, and have governed well; but the general results of the system are not good. No man is fit to exercise absolute

power over a large community. A bad despot crushes his subjects to the earth, and leaves them nothing they can call their own. A good despot teaches his subjects to mind their own private interests, and to leave everything else to the Government.

2. *Constitutional monarchy.* - A powerful aristocracy and a prosperous middle class are not usually disposed to submit to absolute government. They set themselves to limit and define the powers of the monarchy by law. The King retains his position as head of the State, but in all matters of importance he is compelled to ask the advice and consent of persons representing the interests and opinions of his subjects. These persons guide him in choosing his ministers, in raising his revenue, and in every act of his government. The duties of a constitutional king are, on the whole, more difficult than those of a despot; in order to succeed he must be a man of strong judgment, but at the same time impartial and unselfish, and able to co-operate with people whose opinions he does not share. He must refrain from attempting to exercise despotic powers, but he must also beware of becoming a merely titular sovereign. There are few countries where constitutional monarchy is possible; where it is successful, it is a very stable and orderly form of government.

3. *Presidential Republicanism.* Almost all modern Republics have been founded by subjects in rebellion against a king or emperor. The founders of the new government find it necessary to have some central depositary of power; they place the executive under the control of a President, elected for a term of years. Election gives a better guarantee for ability than the

hereditary principle, and a person who holds his office for a limited term may usually be prevented from becoming a despot. But it should be observed that a President is in some ways more powerful than a king. He combines two kinds of power which under a hereditary monarchy are kept separate. He is the head of the State, and as such entitled to peculiar respect; he is also a party leader, dispensing his patronage among his own followers, and framing his policy with a view to the success of his party in the next election.

Aristocracy.

The principle of aristocracy is that the wisest and most considerable people in the community should form a separate class or order, and should exercise a larger measure of political influence than ordinary citizens. This principle is the expression of a tendency which you may see at work in every large body of men, however democratic their notions may be. The character of an aristocracy depends on the method of selection—on the test by which its members are distinguished from their fellow-citizens. On considering the various types of aristocracy, we find that methods of selection have been devised in deference to certain leading ideas which have pervaded and still pervade society.

First, there is the idea of the importance of birth. In primitive society, respect was paid to those who were most directly descended from the common ancestor. Families so connected would form a close aristocracy, into which an outsider could not be received, unless perhaps by adoption. In modern society we do not speak of the common ancestor, but we still defer to the notion that some families are better than others. People give way to the bearer of a well-known name, especially if there is a title attached to the name. Our aristocracy of birth is still to some extent a close one; no merit or favour can confer all the privileges which belong to persons of what is called good birth. But a continual process of adoption goes on, by which the most successful people are ennobled, and their children are added to the number of those who enjoy special consideration on the ground of their birth.

Again, there is the idea of selection by merit and favour. A chief or king confers high rank on those who serve him best; he thus creates an aristocracy of service which he can use to balance the importance of the aristocracy of birth. Modern royalty has so far prevailed over aristocracy of the ancient type, that we now regard all hereditary privileges as lying in the gift of a monarch. When monarchy assumes a constitutional form, such privileges are conferred by responsible ministers, in return for service rendered to the country or to the party in power.

Even where popular election is the only avenue to power, we sometimes see a kind of privileged order formed by natural selection. Thus in America the cleverest party managers form an order strong enough to keep politics pretty much in their own hands. In England, again, the Trade Union leaders are sometimes said to form an aristocracy among working men. But in these cases the term aristocracy is used by analogy.

One advantage of hereditary aristocracy, as it exists among ourselves, is that it supplies a counterpoise to the ambition of individuals who might become despots. Democracy is rather given to looking out for a representative Man and investing him with unlimited powers; but aristocracy is the sworn foe of all unlimited monarchies. The chief reason why our own government has a republican cast is this, that the gentlemen of England do not like to be governed by a masterful individual. Another advantage of aristocracy is, that it supplies a body of persons who have a certain hereditary acquaintance with public affairs. The members of our great families take naturally to the business of government; and they do their work in a creditable manner, though it must be admitted that they are very expensive.

The evil inherent in all aristocracies is that they form a separate interest, which is almost certain to come into conflict with the interest of the community. Privileged persons are apt to look on their privileges as an inheritance which they are bound to transmit unimpaired to their successors; they are unwilling to admit that any of their rights can fairly be considered odious or oppressive. The best members of an aristocracy are thus often induced to make common cause with the worst. Again, the rule of hereditary succession works evil as well as good; where it has prevailed for a long time, a considerable number of hereditary dignities descend to persons quite unfit to exercise power or to make a good use of social influence. Inasmuch as all class distinctions provoke envy and opposition, it requires great skill to maintain a hereditary aristocracy in a country possessing a popular form of government.

Democracy.

The principle of democracy is that all persons who are fit to perform the duties of citizens should have a share in the direction of the State. In ancient communities the scope of this principle was limited by distinctions of blood; thus, a child born at Athens did not become a citizen unless it was the child of a citizen. Modern democracy extends the right of citizenship to all natives of a certain territory, provided they obey the laws and pay taxes if required.

Several reasons may be given for referring questions regarding the State to the whole body of its subjects. No individual or class is fit to exercise uncontrolled power. The members of a government are not likely to understand their business thoroughly unless they are compelled to go out among the people, to study the popular mind, and even to defer a little to popular prejudices. Again, by consulting the people we secure their active co-operation in the work of government. Discipline is best maintained among intelligent men by avoiding arbitrary methods, and by leading them to exercise their own judgment and sense of right. It is also to be observed that the general community forms a tribunal to which we can appeal against the selfish and sectional interests which may seek to prevail against the general good. At the same time, we must not forget that selfish interests may be so combined as to command a majority, and so the principle of democracy may be perverted to wrong purposes.

Democracy is the most hopeful method of government, because it proceeds on the assumption that every citizen may be made fit to exercise power. It is also a difficult method, because the average citizen is slow in his perception of the general interest, and much tempted to use his powers for the advantage of himself or his class. This difficulty is often overlooked by democratic politicians, many of whom are believers in the humanitarian gospel of the eighteenth century. Starting with the belief that man is naturally good, they expect to find a great store of natural virtue in 'the people,' as distinguished from governing persons and classes. In point of fact, the people governed are made of the same clay as the people who govern; no large body of men can be particularly virtuous or particularly wise.

Democracy allows every qualified subject to express an opinion on affairs of State; but it cannot secure that every man's opinion shall influence the action of the State. There is no question of importance on which all the citizens of a State are agreed, and therefore when we speak of 'the will of the people,' we mean the will of the majority for the time being. There are two reasons for allowing the will of the majority to prevail. First, they are on the whole more likely to be right than the minority. If a case is fairly argued, and if the jury is divided, ten against two, the ten are probably in the right. Second, a majority is in most cases physically stronger than a minority. Unless the majority is making a grossly oppressive use of its power, it is better for the minority to submit, lest the majority should be tempted to have recourse to coercion. The rights of the majority are not unlimited in their nature; but they cannot be effectively limited unless by the good sense of those who exercise them.

In practice, it is often difficult to ascertain what the will of the majority really is. Political contests turn on a number of questions which are mixed up together so that no clear decision is given on any one of them. A political majority is always composed of sections, which are only held together by mutual compromise. We say that Liberals or Conservatives are in a majority; and yet there is no single point on which all Liberals or all Conservatives think alike; and a small section is sometimes in a position to decide what the policy of a great party shall be. Representative institutions introduce an additional element of difficulty. The majority of an elected Chamber may represent, and often does represent, a minority of electors. This may happen in spite of the best arrangement you can devise for distributing political power. We must therefore guard ourselves against supposing that the 'rule of the majority' is a simple formula which can be applied with ease to political questions.

Much has been written on the comparative advantages of monarchy and republicanism, the uses and the drawbacks of a hereditary aristocracy, etc. But I am not sure that the politician can derive much profit from such discussions. The form of any actual government is determined, not by abstract reasoning, but by the balance of political powers. Except in times of revolution, no party ever has power enough to change the whole form at once. In ordinary times, when partial changes are proposed (the abolition or reform of the House of Lords, for example), the safest adviser is not the man who reasons most clearly, but the man who can forecast most shrewdly how the Constitution will work when the proposed change has been effected.

CHAPTER VI.

THE CONSTITUTION.

THE Constitution of a State is a collection of rules which determine who are the persons in whom the powers of the State are vested, how their powers are to be exercised, and how the citizens are to be protected against abuse of power.

In many States there is a single document called the Constitution, in which all the most important rules relating to public authorities are contained. An instrument of this kind is usually treated as an exceptional law, not to be altered unless with special precaution. The Congress of the United States, for example, is not permitted to alter the Constitution; amendments can only be introduced by a process which is purposely made difficult.

Our own Constitution is contained in a large number of Royal Charters, Acts of Parliament, Orders of the two Houses, and decisions of the judges; while some of its principles have never been put into legal form at all. It is not specially protected against alteration. We have indeed fundamental laws, the alteration of which would almost amount to a revolution; but these laws are not marked off in any way from the mass of ordinary laws which Parliament alters at discretion.

If you take up a book containing the Constitutions of existing States, you will perceive that they present endless differences of detail, and a certain general similarity of type. In almost all civilised countries, you will find that the powers of government are vested in two classes of persons—professional persons, who spend their lives in some department of the public service; and political persons, whose tenure of power is precarious and dependent on the balance of popular opinion. The relations between the two vary according to the ideas and customs of each country. In Germany the permanent chiefs (the Emperor and his Chancellor) govern the country, subject to the general criticism of the Reichstag, which is elected by universal suffrage. In England the political chiefs (the Prime Minister and his colleagues) govern the country; but they defer continually to the influence of the Queen and other permanent authorities. In the United States, the distinction between permanent and political has been, to a great extent, disregarded. Professional persons cannot count on retaining their offices unless their party remains in power; political persons have quartered themselves on the country as a kind of supplementary permanent service. To pass a judgment on all these modes of government, we should have to enter into a somewhat lengthened inquiry. We shall therefore confine our attention for the present to our own country.

The Permanent Executive.

The Queen is first in dignity and power among our permanent officers; and for that reason her political activity is strictly limited. If her Majesty attends (and we know that she does attend) to her public duties, she must acquire much information, and form tolerably decided opinions, on current questions. But she is debarred from expressing her opinion with the freedom which her subjects enjoy. If the Queen were committed to one side, she might find herself at open variance with the political advisers indicated for her acceptance by the choice of the people. Her influence is very great, but she can retain it only by exercising reserve, caution, and impartiality.

Under the Queen, the routine of public business is carried on by a large body of permanent officers—the military, naval, diplomatic, consular, and civil servants of the Crown. These persons are not excluded from party politics, but they are under a partial restraint, like the Sovereign whose commission they hold: for they serve under political chiefs, chosen from the party in power, and they must co-operate loyally with their chiefs, whatever their own opinion may be. A general may not refuse to march because he thinks the Government ought to have avoided war; and a departmental clerk may not neglect his work because he disapproves of the policy of his chief.

There are of course very many permanent officials in this country, from Under-secretaries of State to policemen and bailiffs. To acquire a correct notion of their various powers and duties, we should have to enter at considerable length into the study of the English Constitution. Confining our attention to matters of general politics, we may observe that politicians should treat the official class with respect and freedom. With respect, because the officials understand, better than any outsider, some important branches of the difficult art of government. With freedom, because officials are apt to introduce needless formality and expense into public business, and may become burdensome to the community if they are not subjected to competent criticism.

Politicians who advocate large reforms should be specially careful to take account of the official element in their schemes. Many modern reforms involve an extension of the sphere of government, which again involves the creation of new offices. Before adopting any scheme of this kind, we should be careful to inquire what additional burden we mean to impose on the community, and whether the advantages of our reform are worth the burden.

The Political Executive.

There are always two or three among the political chiefs of the Government who are placed in power by the popular choice. These two or three persons choose their colleagues from the ranks of their own party, and in this way a Government is formed which makes itself responsible for all the business of the nation. The Government acts as a whole; when a collective resolution has been taken, any member who dissents must either submit or resign. This rule works a certain amount of evil; it almost compels Ministers to use deception; they must appear to be perfectly united, though in fact they hold together only by means of a succession of compromises. But the rule is necessary. If different Ministers could publicly support different opinions, the party in power would be split into sections, and it would be impossible to command a majority in favour of any proposal.

Political Ministers have two very different sets of duties to perform. First, they have their administrative work. Each of them presides over some public office; and though he may not know the detail of the office so well as his permanent assistants, he is responsible for all that is done, and is therefore the person to whom important questions must be referred. In the second place, Ministers have to explain publicly, from day to day, the principles on which they are conducting the government; and this they do in the face of hostile critics, who assume that all their acts are wrong, simply because it is the Government which does them. This duty of public speaking is very important to the nation, because a Government is morally strong only if it carries the judgment of the people along with it. For their own interest also, Ministers must give constant attention to this branch of their work. A Government which has influence over the public mind may commit some administrative errors with impunity; but no amount of administrative merit will save a Government which fails to put its actions in a favourable light before the country.

The Judicature.

There is one branch of the Government which seems to require special mention. I have spoken of the impartiality which becomes a permanent official; but judges and magistrates are under a peculiar obligation in this respect. They ought to act so as to convince every reasonable man that no party or class or individual will receive either more or less than justice at their hands. The measure of justice is not the judge's notion of what is right, but the law, which embodies the best notions of right which our forefathers have been able to reduce to a certain form for enforcement by the public authorities. Our laws are certainly imperfect, and we must endeavour to improve them as opportunity offers. But the law as it stands must be administered with rigid fidelity. All persons and classes ought to be equal before it, the rich man enjoying no privilege, and the poor man pleading no excuse.

There is always a danger that the judges and magistrates may be drawn aside from their duty by political influence. In old times, when judges were appointed by the king and held office at his pleasure, they sometimes strained the law in order to assist the royal prerogative. And in modern times the Bench has sometimes been degraded, in democratically governed countries, by the appointment of partisan judges. Where such appointments are made by popular election, the person elected is peculiarly tempted to be partial and corrupt. It is therefore a principle, accepted by most English statesmen, that judicial appointments should be in the hands of the Government and not of any popular body. The Government may, and usually do, appoint a supporter of their own; but they appoint him quietly in the ordinary course of business, without any of the professions of partisan feeling which are made in a popular election.

The Legislature.

In feudal times, the National Government was constituted very much on the same lines as the Manors which then existed and still exist. Just as the people of a Manor meet with the Lord from time to time in the local courts where the local customs are declared and enforced, so the various estates or orders of people in the kingdom met with the King in the High Court of Parliament, where the laws of the land were declared and enforced; and it was understood that each estate had a right to be consulted in matters concerning itself. The Three Estates of the English realm are the Lords, the Clergy, and the Commons[1]. But as it happened, the greater clergy entered the House of Lords, the lesser clergy obtained the right to vote for members of the House of Commons; so the clergy lost their position as a separate political estate, and our Parliament was organised in two Chambers. And as Parliament has served as the model of free institutions all over the world, the division into two chambers has been accepted as a principle.

There is a theory that the two Houses are equal in authority; and that the House of Lords, being a permanent, hereditary body, is well adapted to check any hasty or revolutionary impulse in the House of Commons. The weakness of this theory was not clearly perceived till 1832; for down to that time the Lords and their friends controlled the great majority of elections to the House of Commons. Since 1832 it has been acknowledged by statesmen of all parties that the House of Commons is the governing house, and that

[1] So also, in France before the Revolution, the States General of the kingdom included the Nobles, the Clergy, and the 'Third Estate.'

the Lords are not justified in resisting a majority of the House of Commons which is supported by a majority of the people. It is precisely when the House of Commons is bent on making some great and sudden change that the Lords have least power to check it. The Irish Church Act of 1869 and the Irish Land Act of 1870 were accepted by the Lords the first time they were sent up by the Commons. The Deceased Wife's Sister Bill has been rejected many times in the Upper House, because it is not supported by a threatening popular agitation.

Our Legislature, then, consists of the House of Commons, which receives from the House of Lords a considerable measure of help, and a limited measure of contradiction. The body thus constituted performs for us two political functions.

First, Parliament is, as old writers say, the Grand Inquest of the nation, to inquire into all matters of public interest. It takes notice of the persons who are called on to advise the Queen in carrying on the Government, and informs the Queen whether these persons are worthy of confidence or not. It requires Ministers to explain from time to time what they are doing, and what reason (if any) they have for doing it. And as Ministers cannot obtain money for the public service except from Parliament, the House of Commons has an annual opportunity of passing all proceedings of the Government under review, and finding out how the public money is spent. Further, Parliament is specially bound to look into grievances—that is, cases in which any subject of the Queen has been deprived or defrauded of his rights. All these inquiries are pursued without any system; for Parliament is not a body of experts, but a mixed body of business men, who do their work under the pressure of outside influences. New claims are constantly being pressed on the attention of the House of Commons, and therefore the House cannot count on being able to get through any programme of work which may be drawn up for its guidance.

Secondly, Parliament has authority to legislate, that is to make, alter, and repeal the rules which subjects of the Queen are compelled to obey. Few members of Parliament possess the knowledge, clearness of mind, and power of expression which are required in the work of legislation. But Parliament can always command the assistance of men specially qualified in these respects; and there is one good reason why the House of Commons, and not any body of experts, should be our legislative authority. If laws are to be effective in a free country they must command the assent of those who are to obey them. Laws made by experts might be very good, but the people would not appreciate their merits. A Bill passed by the House of Commons after a party struggle may be ill conceived and badly expressed; but it embodies some notion of justice which exists as a living belief in the minds of many people throughout the country.

There was a time, not very long ago, when the House of Commons formed and led public opinion, because it was the only place where political questions could be discussed with perfect freedom. At the present time, the House follows public opinion, and does not guide it to any great extent. A Minister who wishes to succeed must obtain what is called a 'popular mandate' in favour of his policy. If the mandate is clear and emphatic, both parties in the House will be eager to gain credit by carrying it out.

The House of Commons differs from many other representative chambers in one important point—its members are not paid. This fact, together with the expensive style of living in this country, must always make it difficult for a poor man to enter the House. The difficulty is met to some extent by private subscriptions in aid of 'labour representatives' and others; but there are those who think that we must go further and provide a sufficient salary for every member of Parliament. Before accepting this proposal, we shall do well to study the experience of other countries. In France, and in the United States, reformers have been known to complain that payment of members tends to increase the numbers of professional politicians so-called, who live by working the machinery of party. Popular representatives are elected to check the paid servants of the public; but if the representatives themselves are paid, they are apt to look at things from the salaried official's point of view.

Local Authorities.

Besides the authorities of the Central Government, we have a great variety of officers and Boards to manage the affairs of parishes, counties, and other areas of local Government. Some of these areas—as, for example, the Union—have been created by Parliament, others are more ancient in their origin than Parliament itself. The vestry of a country parish is the direct successor of the popular assembly of primitive times.

The distribution of power between central and local authorities is a matter calling for the exercise of political judgment. It is for the central government to mark out the limits within which inferior bodies are to act, and the general principles which are to guide them. Within their own sphere, local authorities must have a certain measure of independence, a certain liberty in trying experiments on their own responsibility. This is not a question which admits of very definite treatment. There is a time to centralise, and a time to decentralise; it is the business of statesmen and municipal leaders to see that both principles are kept in view in arranging the machinery of government.

In studying an imperial constitution, we have to take account of the local rights of communities which are so composed and so territorially situated that they may be regarded as separate states or nations. Rights of this kind are not to be confounded with those of merely municipal bodies. Liverpool is almost as populous as New Zealand; but the Liverpool Corporation is a merely subordinate body, while the New Zealand Government is an independent centre of politics and legislation. The Irish demand for Home Rule, as stated by Mr. Butt, was not a demand for local self-government, in the ordinary sense of the term; it was a demand for the creation of a new political centre.

The relation between politics and constitutional law is well described in Bagehot's *English Constitution* and Dicey's *Law of the Constitution*: the actual machinery of the constitution is described in Alpheus Todd's *Parliamentary Government in England*.

CHAPTER VII.

ELECTIONS.

The functions of the modern State are so numerous that the citizens are compelled to leave the work of government to a class of persons who are supposed to be specially qualified for it. In free countries, the persons who make and execute the laws derive their authority from popular election. To give a complete account of all existing modes of choosing representatives would be an immense undertaking; but we may obtain some useful notions on this subject, by taking a rapid general survey of the rules which apply to parliamentary elections in our own country.

Electoral Qualifications.

In primitive society, free birth and capacity to bear arms usually qualify a man to take part in the deliberations of the tribal assembly.

In feudal times, every English freeholder (that is, every man holding land by any of the more honourable kinds of tenure) had a right to take part in the county court for electing knights of the shire. In the reign of Henry VI, Parliament restricted the right to freeholders whose land was worth 40s. a year. In the course of time, 40s. came to be a small sum, and the number of freeholders entitled to vote was very large. Till 1832 there was only this one franchise in the counties. Among the boroughs, on the other hand, there was a great diversity of franchises. In some, the owners of freehold 'burgage tenements' voted; in others, the members of the Corporation; in others, again, all inhabitants paying scot and lot.

The Reform Act of 1832 set aside some of these ancient qualifications, and introduced a considerable body of new electors, by extending the franchise to all persons who occupied property of a certain value. The Reform Act of 1867 did away with distinctions of value in boroughs, by admitting all householders and lodgers; and this equal rule has been extended to counties by the Act of 1884. As the nett result of these changes we now have an electorate almost as large in proportion to population as the electorate of countries where Universal Suffrage is the rule. But it is important to remark, that in France and elsewhere, Universal Suffrage has been established in deference to a theory; in this country we have reached Household Suffrage by a gradual process.

Each extension of the franchise has been resisted on grounds which are worth considering. First, it has been argued that a narrow franchise is necessary to maintain the legitimate influence of property and education. This appears to me to be a mistake. A man of property and culture will always have influence with his neighbours, if he chooses to work for it. If rich men try to restrict electoral rights in order to keep up their influence, they make it evident that what they desire is to have influence *without* working for it.

Again, it has been argued that by extending the franchise we should admit many persons not well qualified to exercise it. There is some truth in this objection ; but those who urge it have done great harm by confining their attention to one class of the community. They tell us that the average labourer is imperfectly instructed in politics, and liable to be swayed by interest and prejudice. True ; and so is the average graduate of Oxford. If the franchise were given as the reward of proved capacity, it would be given to a small body, selected from all classes. But we have no authority which could be trusted to make the selection, and therefore we admit all classes on an equal footing, without attempting to draw an invidious and misleading distinction between professional men, tradesmen, and labouring men.

It has also been said, that by extending the franchise, we have thrown the preponderance of voting power in every constituency into the hands of a single class—the labouring class. This would be a serious consideration if labouring people should come to think that their interest is separate from and hostile to the interests of other classes. I venture to say that the mass of labouring people will not take this view of politics, so long as the leaders of public opinion do their duty in a fearless, just, and considerate manner.

Electoral Districts.

Down to 1832, electoral districts were arranged on historical lines. Every ancient county, and every ancient borough, with few exceptions, sent two members to the House of Commons ; the 14,000 freeholders of Yorkshire sent two and no more, while there is said to have been a Cornish borough where two members represented one elector. In 1832 and again in 1867 partial remedies were provided for these inequalities. Finally, in 1885, the matter was taken up on general principles. By far the greater part of the United Kingdom is now divided into single-member districts of approximately equal size. Before deciding to adopt this scheme of division, Parliament had to consider the merits of three competing plans for the distribution of electoral power.

1. There is the plan known in France as *Scrutin de liste*, by which large districts are created, returning several members each. Each elector has as many votes as there are members to be returned; so that the majority in each district may return all the members for the district. This plan has not commanded any large measure of support in this country.

2. There are various plans of Proportional Representation. According to this scheme, large districts are taken, or the whole country may be treated as one district. Each elector has one vote, but he is allowed to vote for several candidates, marking the order of his preference. Elaborate provision is made for transferring votes *from* candidates who obtain more than the number necessary to return them, and *to* candidates who obtain less than the necessary number of first preferences. The ultimate result is, that Liberals and Conservatives are represented in proportion to their numbers, while any section of opinion can secure a representative if it can poll the number of votes necessary to return one candidate.

This plan is more ideally just than any other, but it has not received much support in this country, and that for two reasons. In the first place, it takes a little trouble to understand the system and to meet the objections commonly made against it. 'Practical' politicians usually object to anything which cannot be made plain at once; they deal in broad generalities, and refuse to attend to details. In the second place, proportional representation is not favourable to that kind of rough compromise which is the soul of our national politics. Members are sent to Parliament, not merely to represent some opinion or interest, but to co-operate in carrying on the public business. If members were returned by small homogeneous bodies of voters, they would be more strictly bound by pledges than they are at present, and it might be more difficult to secure a working majority in the House of Commons. I do not myself regard this as an insurmountable objection; but it is the objection which has weight with those popular leaders of opinion who have declared against proportional representation.

3. There is the plan actually adopted, of single-member districts of equal or approximately equal size. This is in some ways the roughest plan of all. It leaves every local minority entirely unrepresented; and the local distribution of opinion is so much a matter of accident, that a party may secure a number of local victories and so come into power with a large majority in the House of Commons, though its majority among the electors may be small or even nonexistent. But while we recognise the force of these abstract objections, we must not make too much of them. The scheme of single-member districts contains some valuable elements. It preserves the constituency as a local unit, and this ought to have a good effect, if the con-

stituencies preserve their independence and send up the best men they can find, not the men who find most favour in the eyes of party managers in London. Again, the comparative smallness of a single-member district tends to reduce the expense and trouble of an election.

Candidates and Members.

Any male British subject of full age may be chosen a member of the House of Commons: to this general rule there are only a very few exceptions. Peers are disqualified, because they belong to that Estate which is represented in the House of Lords. Clergymen of the established Church are disqualified, because they once possessed the right of taxing themselves in Convocation. Roman Catholic priests are disqualified; other dissenting ministers are eligible. Lunatics and criminals are not eligible; and certain special disabilities are imposed on persons who have been found guilty of corrupt practices. Atheists and agnostics are eligible, and the law of parliamentary oaths no longer debars them from sitting and voting. Another law restricting the number of candidates is that which compels each candidate to pay a share of the returning officers' charges.

A candidate may stand on his own merits as an independent politician, but in the vast majority of cases he is and must be the nominee of a party. If none but 'independent members' were returned to the House of Commons, they would have to fuse themselves into parties before any business could be done. The selection of a party candidate raises some general questions of considerable importance.

How should the candidate of a party be chosen? Any elector may suggest a name; any candidate may come forward and offer himself with or without introduction; and the strength of the party may be divided. It is to prevent this result that the institution popularly known as the Caucus has been adopted in many places by both our great parties. The institution is still young and has not hitherto worked quite smoothly. We have not attained—let us hope we never may attain—that perfection of party discipline which some zealous politicians would like to see. It is always possible to appeal to the general body of electors against any limited Association or Committee. We are almost all agreed in holding that a Caucus is entitled to respect only if it is (1) Honestly worked; and (2) Fairly representative of all sections of the party. If it does not satisfy these two conditions it is a nuisance, and ought to be suppressed.

If it be asked, what kind of men should be preferred as candidates? the only answer is: those who are best qualified to understand and take part in the business of the House of Commons. It is not necessary that a member of Parliament should be a fine speaker, or that he should be able to make telling attacks on the other side. It is necessary that he should have the knowledge and experience which enable a man to vote intelligently on questions of law and government. Having regard to the bitterness and the tedious length of our party conflicts, electors will do well to avoid candidates who are excitable, or wanting in physical stamina.

Ought the persons who choose a candidate to bind him by definite instructions? There should certainly be a clear understanding as to the terms on which a member is elected. He cannot be too explicit in laying his views before the electors, and if, after entering Parliament, a serious difference arises between himself and his constituents, he may feel bound in honour to resign. It is unfortunate that our law does not permit a member to resign, except by the roundabout process of applying for an office under the Crown. But while a candidate is bound to defer to the opinion of the electors, they must allow him a considerable measure of independence. A member of Parliament ought to be a man of special knowledge; he ought also to be a man of character, who can be trusted to use his own judgment. Some electors like to multiply test questions, and to compel candidates to swear adherence to every article of an elaborate party programme. If these tactics were generally adopted, we should have a very 'safe' body of candidates, and a very inferior body of representatives. Electors must remember that a candidate is always tempted to suppress or deny his opinions in order to conciliate them; and they should beware of making the temptation too strong.

Corrupt Practices.

Many electors think that a seat in Parliament is a social distinction, for which a candidate should be prepared to pay; and in many places an election has long been regarded as an opportunity out of which any citizen who is so minded should be able to make some profit. So much evil has been wrought by corrupt customs that an Act has been passed, prescribing rigorously what each candidate may spend, and how he may spend it. We may hope for some good result from the operation of this stringent law, but we must observe that there are some kinds of corruption which the law can do little to check. It is not easy to deal with places where there is a corrupt understanding between Liberals and Conservatives—neither party choosing to set the law in motion against the other. Nor is it possible to prevent rich men from 'nursing' a constituency; a man may spend large sums in a place for a series of years, and then stand for Parliament on the strength of his popularity. Such practices can only be checked by promoting the sternest sort of political honesty among the electors.

There is a savour of corruption in many of the appeals which politicians make to their supporters. Each party is tempted to prove its 'generosity' by promising to confer great benefits on a particular class or interest; and it is often difficult to draw the line between those who support a measure because they think it just, and those who support it because they think they will gain something by it. There is no safeguard against this form of corruption, except the safeguard we provide by cultivating an impartial method of treating public questions.

Secret Voting.

To take and number the votes of a large constituency is a difficult process. In going through this process, we have to solve a good many mechanical problems; we have also to solve a moral problem of the highest importance. Ought the voters to declare their preference openly? Secret voting is now the rule in this and other countries, and this rule has been adopted for three reasons.

1. Secret voting is favourable to order on the polling day.

2. Secret voting discourages certain forms of corruption. A person who gives money for the promise of a vote knows that he and the voter are both dishonest. He will not risk his money if the other knave may cheat him by voting secretly against him. Against this advantage must be set a corresponding disadvantage. It is now possible for an elector to sell his vote to both sides: in 1880 there were 127 persons in one English borough who actually did so.

3. The strongest argument in favour of secret voting is that it prevents intimidation. A tradesman wishes to vote Liberal, but the local Conservatives threaten to withdraw their custom. A Dissenter wishes to vote Conservative, but his chapel friends threaten to boycott him. In these and other cases the Ballot enables the voter to record his real opinion.

The protection afforded by the Ballot is unhappily very partial. No law can prevent landlords and land-leaguers from inquiring how an elector means to vote. If the elector fences with the question, he is set down as hostile; nothing will serve but a point-blank answer. If the answer is false, the elector is committed to a course of deception; he must wear the wrong colour and attend the wrong meeting; he must groan if he is on the winning side, and cheer if his candidate fails.

When society is in a healthy state, a man will be able to vote against any individual or league without ill-feeling on either side. As soon as the Ballot can be dispensed with, we ought certainly to dispense with it. In recording his vote, an elector acts not only for himself but for others[1]. If I vote Liberal, I am doing my best to hand over the Empire to a Liberal Government for five or six years. If the Liberals come in and misconduct themselves in office, my neighbours ought to know that I am one of the parties who are responsible.

Where honest electors, irrespective of party, are determined that no man shall suffer for expressing his honest opinion, intimidation is impossible.

For the details of our electoral system, the only safe guides are the books on election law, such as Rogers on Elections; see also Sir W. Anson, *Law and Custom of the Constitution*, Part I. Proportional representation is advocated in Hare on Representation, and in a little volume by Sir J. Lubbock in the Imperial Parliament Series. The arguments for and against secret voting may be found in the debates of the Ballot Act of 1872.

---

[1] This statement is denied by a friendly critic, who argues that the franchise ceased to be a trust when it was extended to all householders. If the franchise is not a trust, I do not see why an elector should be forbidden to sell his vote.

CHAPTER VIII.

POLITICAL IDEALS.

GOOD government encourages virtue, industry, and public spirit in each individual citizen, and good will among the various classes of which the community is composed. This very general statement may serve to express the ideal which all wise politicians keep in view. To give precision to our general notion of good government, we shall find it useful to examine some more particular notions which constantly recur in political reasoning. Those who approve of a certain form or method of government usually tell us that it is orderly, just, progressive, free, and so forth. Each of these terms has a definite meaning; each of them indicates some definite object at which government ought to aim.

Order.

The most essential condition of social well-being is this, that men should abstain from injuring and abusing one another, and from disobeying or evading the laws made for the general benefit. In a large body of men, order can only be maintained by the combined operation of many agencies, which may be grouped under two heads.

First, there must be repressive agencies for the prevention and punishment of disorder. Every community contains a proportion of self-willed persons, who can only be governed by threats of coercion. For the benefit of these persons, we must make our threats (that is, our penal laws) as clear as possible; and we must see that force is always at hand to make our threats effectual. Sentimental politicians are apt to argue as if just laws would render all coercion unnecessary; but this is a mistake. Many men are so ignorant, so fanatical, or so eager for their own advantage, that they will not obey any law whatever unless they know that disobedience will be punished.

Second, there must be educating agencies, so that each citizen may learn to understand and respect the law. Good government does not reduce the individual to the state of an automaton; it increases his personal worth by making him co-operate with the State for the general good. Every man so educated is a centre of order; he helps to form a sound public opinion, which checks disorder before it has time to display itself in action.

Liberty.

Liberty is a word of negative meaning, denoting merely absence of restraint. Men usually object to any restraint which can possibly be dispensed with, and therefore the word liberty has always an attractive and inspiring sound. There are two kinds of freedom which seem to be essential to social improvement.

First, the community must be free from the domination of alien powers. Thus we say that Greece became a free country when her people ceased to be subject to Turkish rule. People who are in the early stages of civilisation sometimes derive benefit from being governed by a superior race. The condition of a Zulu in the colony of Natal is certainly in many respects better than that of a Zulu living under his native institutions. Whether a nation is fit for freedom is a question of fact, and sometimes a difficult question to decide.

Secondly, progress is impossible unless the individual is free from unnecessary interference on the part of the government. All political authorities are given to meddle with matters which they do not quite understand, and to suppress or discourage varieties of opinion and conduct. Governing minorities and governing majorities are equally prone to this mistake. We must therefore take care to preserve for each individual a sphere within which he may think and act freely, on his own sole responsibility.

The arguments in favour of individual liberty are so strong that we can afford to discard some fallacious reasons which are not unfrequently used to recommend it. One or two of these fallacies seem to require special notice.

Many writers have advocated liberty on the ground that man is naturally virtuous. They assume that if the restraint of our imperfect laws were removed, nature would prompt men to act rationally and to live at peace with one another. This argument proceeds on a partial and incorrect view of human nature. Men are by nature both good and bad. We favour liberty because it enables the good to become better, and also because it leaves the bad to encounter the consequences of their faults.

Again, it is said that certain acts of a man's life are 'self-regarding' acts, and as such exempt from the interference of society. This is the thesis of Mill's eloquent essay on Liberty, but I do not think his argument will bear examination. No act of the individual can be wholly indifferent to society; nor are we ever justified in denying the right of society to interfere, on the ground that what we are doing concerns nobody but ourselves. To take an example: we deny that the State has a right to interfere with a man who gets quietly drunk in his own house. Why? Not because the man is doing a 'self-regarding' act: he is in fact committing an offence against society by wasting his substance, and making himself unfit to perform any social duty. But the State cannot touch him without assuming an inquisitorial power to interfere in domestic concerns: and the State is not wise enough to be trusted with such powers.

Justice.

No term is more freely employed in current politics than 'Justice'; and no term seems to stand more in want of definition. If we wish to be accurate, we must carefully notice the different meanings attached to this word. There are, as it seems to me, three kinds of justice, each of which has its own place in civilised society.

1. Justice according to law. This consists in the firm application of established rules to all cases and persons alike. Every judge and public officer must carry out the law faithfully, and may not refrain from doing so because he thinks the policy of the law doubt-

ful. Every citizen is bound to obey the law, whether it suits his own interests or not. If *one* man may say 'This law seems to me unfair, therefore I will not obey it,' *every* man may say the same of any law, and our one security against disorder would be broken down.

2. The legislator administers a wider and more flexible kind of justice than the magistrate; for in making laws we do not merely apply principles already laid down; we may also introduce new principles, and provide machinery for giving effect to them. In exercising this power, a wise legislator will give equal consideration to all persons and claims. He will avoid the creation of anything in the nature of privilege, whether it is claimed by the rich on the ground of their wealth, or by the poor on the ground of their poverty. He will endeavour to apply, as far as possible, the same standard of right to all.

3. By far the most searching and complete kind of justice is that which is done by righteous individuals within the sphere of their personal action and influence. A just man renders willing obedience to the laws of his country. Even if he thinks a certain law should be altered, he respects legal rights so long as they are legal[1]. He gives impartial consideration to the claims of others; he scrupulously gives full value, in work or money, for what he receives. He is careful not to exaggerate his own claims on others. He 'stands aloof from injustice,' and refuses to participate in the advantages of any social arrangement which he knows to be unfair. Such are the characteristics of moral

[1] The cases where an individual honestly thinks it his duty to disobey the law, will be considered in another chapter.

justice, which is far more perfect in its nature than political justice can ever become.

It is important to observe that political justice is not and never can be absolute justice. If the State proposes to do absolute justice, it will require perfect knowledge and unlimited power. But the knowledge of the State is very imperfect, and its power must be kept within strict limits, unless we wish to see it become an inquisitorial tyranny. There are many wrongs which the State cannot redress: there are many duties which it cannot enforce. This general truth applies with special force to the more intimate relations of life. The State cannot do complete justice as between husband and wife, landlord and tenant, employer and employed.

Politicians are apt to assume that justice is very simple and easy to discover. When difficult questions arise about property—the Irish Land Question, for example—it is supposed that any honest man can see at once what 'justice' requires. In fact, justice is almost always obscure and difficult to work out; the greater a man's knowledge of social facts, the more unwilling he will be to play the part of 'a judge and a divider' among his fellows.

There are some who call for justice because they think that if justice were done we should all be pretty well off. This is, I fear, a mistaken impression. If strict justice were done, you and I would probably be in a somewhat uncomfortable position. We should receive only what we have earned by honest service; and we should have to pay a full penalty for the ill we have done and the good we have neglected to do.

When men demand justice, they very often mean only the removal of some particular inequality which they have found to be a hardship: they do not consider what would be the effect of a thoroughgoing application of the principle.

The Rights of Man.

In the eighteenth century the theory of political justice was freely worked out on the basis of the humanitarian belief which then prevailed. It was asserted that each man, by the mere fact of his birth, came into possession of certain rights, and especially of the right to live and to pursue his own happiness. If society failed to secure to each individual the full measure of the rights of man, then the individual would be justified in breaking up society. To perceive the true character of this theory, we must pay careful heed to the meaning of the words we use.

A right is a claim recognised and, if necessary, enforced by the State. Every right implies two parties — the person who makes a claim, and the person or body of persons against whom it is made. Thus, my right to my house is a claim to have exclusive possession; the claim is made against all my neighbours. If one of my neighbours should trespass, the State will permit and assist me to enforce my claim by turning him out. Observe that a claim is called a right, not because it is just, but because it is supported by the force of Law. Thus, a wife has a strong *claim* to be kindly treated by her husband. But she has no *right* to kind treatment, because the law cannot compel a man to be kind. She has a right to a sufficient maintenance, because the law can and will compel her husband to provide her with food and clothing.

When we speak of 'moral rights' we mean claims which would, in our opinion, be converted into rights if our legislation were guided by moral considerations. When we speak of 'natural rights' we mean claims which would be converted into rights if Parliament took the same view of things in general as we do. 'Moral rights' and 'natural rights' are purely ideal; they have no existence in the actual world of politics and law. If a certain claim is put forward as a right, the proper question is, Can it be legally enforced? If it cannot, the law-reformer may proceed to consider the question, Ought this claim to be made enforceable by law? Some may object to this precise legal way of reasoning out the case. But the term 'right' is a legal term; and people like it just because it is legal—because it conveys the notion of a decree or law by which somebody is to be compelled to do something for them. If politicians will use legal language, they must use it with some measure of precision.

Let us apply the foregoing definitions to the simplest of the 'rights of man'—the right to live. Whole systems have been based on this 'right,' the existence of which is supposed to be too clear to require any proof. Yet no such right exists in any civilised country, and we should have to consider the matter before making it part of our law. If every man has a right to live, enforceable against the community, it is plain that nobody need fear want, at least for some little time to come. Why, for instance, should a peasant hesitate to marry early, and settle three or four sons on his little holding? If each son has an 'equal, inalienable right to live,' the landlord or the State will be bound to see that they do not starve.

It must always be remembered that 'my rights' are simply 'the duties which I can compel other people to perform.' If you look at it in that way, you see at once why the rights of the individual must be kept within strict limits, and why it is impossible to admit that a man acquires any rights by merely being born in a particular place.

Equality.

Absolute equality is of course an impossible ideal. The differences between men are so great, that no power can make and keep them equal. But in all political justice there are certain elements of equality.

First, there is equality before the law. It would be wrong if a judge or public officer were to deal with men differently, according to their rank or wealth, their political opinions or their social popularity; or if laws were passed to benefit one set of people at the expense of another.

Again, there ought to be, among citizens of the same community, a certain equality of political consideration. It is not true to say that one man is as good as another; but we may hold that each man has an equally good claim to be heard on questions which concern him, and to have his interest taken into account in deciding such questions.

The equality which should prevail among us is not the equality of men standing each on his own rights, and jealously watching one another; but rather the equality which exists among friends. A good citizen should be neither overbearing nor condescending, neither mutinous nor abject. We are all alike citizens; the greatest of us can be nothing more, and the meanest should be made to feel that he is nothing less.

Fraternity.

Whether all men are united by a common descent or not is a disputed question. In any case, they may well desire to cultivate brotherly feeling among themselves. But fraternity can hardly yet be accepted as a political ideal; for fraternal sympathy, where it exists, is spontaneous and cannot be directly promoted by political means.

'Sympathy' is the keynote which every orator and popular writer tries to strike. It is often struck, very skilfully, by party men, who work on the emotions of men in the mass, in order to obtain their votes. We must therefore observe that while sympathy is an element in statesmanship, it is only one of many elements in the character of a true statesman. The foolish nurse gives the patient whatever he longs for; the doctor notes his patient's wish for this or that as one of the symptoms of his malady. In like manner, the emotional politician identifies himself with some class or body of people so completely that he makes their demands the measure of political justice. The true statesman can understand and enter into every honest aspiration, however unreasonable. But his sympathy with his fellow-men does not rouse him to the point of believing all that they say, or approving of all that they do.

The greatest happiness of the greatest number.

This is a formula which has done good service in the hands of the utilitarians. It reminds us that the test of social institutions is the condition of the greatest number, and not the condition of any selected class.

But we must always distinguish between immediate happiness, which consists in the satisfaction of desire, and ultimate happiness, which is a state of material and moral well-being only to be attained by hard work, and by the sacrifice of immediate happiness.

As soon as we attempt to make a close application of the formula under discussion, we find that it is only a rough statement of an obvious truth, and not really a guiding principle. There are, as we have seen, two kinds of happiness, and measures which make for the one kind are hostile to the other. Again, there is no standard of quantity or quality by means of which one kind of happiness can be compared with another; and no argument founded on such comparison can be clearly verified. Suppose a young men's society has a sum of money to spend. Half the members vote for spending it in books, and half for spending it in beer. Now suppose that the men who vote for beer are men who never read, while those who vote for books do sometimes drink beer. In this case the 'greatest happiness of the greatest number' is promoted by buying beer. But it would be much wiser to buy books for all that.

If you set out to promote the happiness of your fellow-men, you must carefully consider whether you are going to give them what ought to make them happy, or what does in fact make them happy.

The value of Ideals.

Our examination of popular ideals has led us to some rather disappointing results. Phrases which are used every day as if they had one clear meaning, turn out to be really quite ambiguous. But if these phrases are unsatisfactory, it does not follow that we are to have no ideals at all. The inference I prefer to draw is this: that we must leave phrases for facts; we must try to be good citizens, and beware of abstract politics.

The abstract politician is busy among us to-day, in Europe and America. He moves blindly among facts which he does not see and men whom he cannot manage. He deals with formulæ as if they were realities; and this is one reason why our political debates are so often without significance. For instance, when a Coercion Bill for Ireland is introduced into the House of Commons, it is promoted in the name of 'order,' and resisted in the name of 'liberty.' But these abstract terms have but little meaning for those who use them most readily. The friends of 'order,' persist in governing Ireland by methods which are well adapted to perpetuate disorder. As for the friends of 'liberty,' it is enough to say that they are the inventors of that abominable form of social tyranny known as 'boycotting.'

The mother of a well-managed household does not begin the day with eloquent remarks about the good old cause of liberty and order. She keeps close to the small facts of character and circumstance which make up family life. She tries to be accurate, even-handed, even-tempered; and so her children become independent and orderly and helpful. In the same way, a sensible politician keeps close to the people among whom he lives. If he can succeed in clearing their minds and in penetrating them with the spirit of justice and good-will, the political forms of justice will emerge naturally, without the disturbance which is caused by the application of a rigid formula to human affairs.

See J. S. Mill's *Essay on Liberty*, and Sir J. F. Stephen, *Liberty, Equality, Fraternity.*

CHAPTER IX.

PARTIES AND PARTY GOVERNMENT.

A PARTY is a body of citizens who agree in desiring to see the business of legislation and government carried on in a particular way. A party is said to be in power when it places its leading members at the head of the goverment; a party not in power is usually said to be in opposition, and devotes itself to more or less hostile criticism of the acts of the government. Leaders of opposition are expected to restrain their followers from obstruction, and to direct attention to those acts of the government which are really open to objection. If the opponents of a government succeed in placing it in a minority on an important question, they are expected to undertake the formation of a new government.

A party is held together partly by agreement in opinion, partly by interest and personal association; it has a kind of corporate existence; it demands from its members an allegiance similar to the allegiance which they owe to the State. It has no legal power over its members, but it exercises an effective control over their words and actions.

For obvious reasons, politicians tend to divide themselves into Conservatives and Reformers; but this is a very rough division, and we should have some difficulty in applying it to the actual state of parties. In order to obtain some accurate notions of this important subject we may endeavour to survey the history and the present position of the parties now competing for power in our own country.

The Tories.

Toryism is the creed of those who have never surrendered the old Catholic doctrine of authority. They start with the belief that man is a disorderly creature, requiring both political and ecclesiastical guidance. They hold that the monarchy, the aristocracy, and the Church are appointed by Divine Providence to afford the guidance we require. They take a high view of the duty which persons in authority owe to the people; but they do not admit that the people may enforce this duty or freely criticise the manner of its performance. Their reliance is not on the judgment of the people, but on their loyalty—that is, the readiness of the people to recognise and submit to a genuine authority.

True Toryism will always have an attraction for chivalrous minds; but it is weak in its hold on facts. It accepts Charles I as the model of a Patriot King, and even worships him as a Royal Saint. It ignores the fact that royal authority is vested in fallible persons, who must be held to their duties as strictly as ordinary men. It goes on teaching that the Church is 'the nation, ecclesiastically considered,' although a large part of the nation is outside the Church altogether. Toryism, therefore, tends more and more to become a sentiment rather than a belief. It breathes historic air, and has no vital connexion with modern society.

The Conservatives.

The transition from Toryism to Conservatism was ably managed by Sir Robert Peel. He accepted the Liberal principle of toleration by admitting Papists to political rights. He was himself a member of the new aristocracy of capital which he helped to raise to an equality with the old landed aristocracy. He felt that Tory principles were rendered impossible by the Reform Act of 1832 ; and he took the lead in shaping the Conservative principles which replaced the old faith.

The Conservatives do not pretend to maintain the doctrine of authority. They are faithful to the monarchy, the aristocracy, and the Church ; but they defend these institutions on grounds of expediency. They would like to erect safeguards to prevent democracy from meddling with certain interests of high social importance; but they recognise the supremacy of public opinion. They object to all fundamental change; but they make large concessions to the spirit of reform.

Conservatism is eminently respectable, but it wants character and purpose. A Conservative seldom knows how many Liberal principles he means to accept and carry out. He wants to keep as much of the old Constitution as he can, but how much can be kept is a question which he leaves to his leaders to determine ; and his leaders are rather apt to disconcert and demoralise him by sudden changes of front—as when Mr. Disraeli declared for Household Suffrage in 1867.

After undergoing one or two trials of this sort, Conservatives have learned to sit loose to the traditional part of their creed.

The Whigs.

In the reign of Charles II, the friends of absolute monarchy came to be known as Tories, that is, Irish ruffians—probably because the Stuarts raised troops among the wild Irish when they needed help against their English subjects. About the same time, the friends of parliamentary monarchy came to be known as Whigs—that is, sour Scotch fanatics—because of their connexion with the Presbyterians in the North. The Whigs triumphed in the Revolution of 1688 and in the establishment of the Hanoverian dynasty; and Tory principles were proscribed, as savouring of Jacobitism, until they were revived in a new form under George III.

The Whigs were Protestant but not Puritan. They discarded the notion of absolute authority; they regarded the Constitution as a system of checks and balances. They upheld the monarchy, but they would not allow the King to act except through Ministers possessing the confidence of Parliament. They upheld the Church, but they took away from it the power of independent action and made it a department of the State. They maintained the House of Lords, but they prevented that House from becoming a close aristocracy, by preserving the right of the Crown (that is, of the Government) to create peers at will. The leading Whig principle was a principle of consent and compromise. There was to be no taxation without representation; no legal burden was to be imposed on the subject unless by the consent of the several orders of subject persons represented in Parliament.

Like the Tories, the Whigs were a party with definite doctrines; and therefore they could not hope to subsist under modern political conditions. With a wide popular suffrage, and perfect freedom of speech and writing, no great party can afford to have a definite creed. A majority can be made up only by combining people of very various opinions; and each party must be ready to gain votes by adopting any principle which seems to work well, or to command popular support. Such are the conditions under which the name of Whig has been gradually supplanted by the vaguer name of Liberal.

The Liberals.

The name of Liberal was first introduced into politics by the friends of constitutional monarchy in France about the beginning of this century[1]. At first it was not a popular name. Monarchists disliked it because it was associated with popular government and religious toleration (which they took to be the same as religious indifference). Revolutionary politicians disliked it because Liberals treated the monarchy and the Church with respect, and took but little account of 'the rights of man.' But the term Liberal was so general and so well sounding that it was bound to succeed. About the time when Conservatism came to denote a firm but not immoderate attachment to existing institutions, Liberalism came to denote an enlightened but not im-

[1] It is said that the first organised party which adopted the name was the Spanish Liberal party of 1808.

moderate desire of progress and reform. Respectable politicians usually lay claim to both names; thus a Conservative government 'professes to pursue a truly liberal policy'; and a Liberal government assures us that its measures are 'conservative in the best sense of the word.'

Liberalism has presided over the political changes of the last sixty years. Its function has been to hold the balance between authoritative monarchy and aristocracy on the one hand, and authoritative democracy on the other. How it performs this function may best be shown by considering separately the three great principles on which European Liberals are tolerably unanimous.

1. Religious toleration. In Ireland, the English Government (a liberal body, though governing by despotic methods) endeavours to treat all creeds alike. In this endeavour it encounters the opposition of the Protestant oligarchy, in whose interest the Established Church was once maintained; and it has to keep back the zeal of the Catholic priests and peasantry, many of whom would like to extirpate Protestantism. In France, the Liberals are always trying to moderate between aggressive clericalism on the one hand and aggressive secularism on the other.

2. Popular government. Liberalism has extended political rights, first to the middle class and then to the labouring class, without regard to the Tory doctrine of authority or the Whig doctrine of checks and balances. It has been gradually led to throw a great preponderance of voting power into the hands of the labouring class, but it has not done so in deference to

a theory. Lord Russell and Mr. Bright would probably have rejected the notion of a 'natural right' to the franchise; they argued the question on grounds of expediency and business-like fairness, not on grounds of abstract equality.

3. Freedom of trade. In England, France, and Germany Liberalism is identified with the system of free trade. Authoritative Toryism favours protection in the interest of landlords, and attempts to encourage industry by means of bounties and privileges. Authoritative democracy favours the same mistaken system, because many labouring people think they can keep up their own wages by excluding foreign competition—or, in other words, by restricting the liberty of their neighbours in order to make work for themselves. In France, in the United States, and in some of our colonies, the masses of working people are protectionist at heart. In our own country, the democratic argument for protection has been little heard. The battle of free trade was fought out on the question of the Corn Laws, which were maintained in the supposed interest of the landlord and the capitalist farmer. But it is worth observing that 'fair trade' (that is, protection) is an article in the new creed of Tory democracy in England and Parnellite democracy in Ireland.

The Radicals.

In the year 1819 the Government of Lord Liverpool was using every effort to repress manifestations of popular discontent, and to put a stop to the agitation for parliamentary reform. Some of the friends of reform began to find that the old name of Whig was not strong enough; they preferred to call themselves Radical Reformers. Since that time the name of Radical has been used to denote those Liberal politicians who are most in favour of large changes in our laws and methods of government. By slow degrees the milder Liberals have been won over to Radical ideas. Some have been converted, some have been coerced; and it seems not unlikely that the party struggle of the immediate future will be a struggle between Liberal Radicalism, on the one hand, and Tory democracy, which is a kind of Radicalism, on the other. But Tory democracy is as yet so undeveloped that we confine our attention for the present to the Liberal variety of Radicalism.

The Radicals are strong in numbers, in good intentions, and popular sympathies; but their principles are still indefinite and confused. Most of them have adopted (unconsciously and without any process of reasoning) the humanitarian doctrine of continental democracy. They are apt to assume that men are naturally good, and will behave well if they are allowed to have all their own way. Radicals usually trace all the evils of society to unjust laws and defective institutions; and they overrate the results which may be obtained by changing the laws so as to give free play to the instincts of the average man. They advise us to place 'unlimited confidence in the people'—that is, in ourselves; they make the 'will of the people' a kind of sacred authority, although the will of the people means only the will of the majority.

Radicals are eager to discover and point out imperfections in our social system, and herein they do well.

But criticism must be qualified with modesty and goodwill; otherwise it will breed an envious discontent. We must beware of the common delusion that *we* could set the world right in a short time, if we only had unlimited power. This is the delusion of all authoritative politicians, whether Tory or Radical.

All Radicals seem to agree in accepting two propositions. (1) Society as it exists is not in a satisfactory state. Wealth and power and knowledge are concentrated in the hands of the few; and the life of the mass of mankind is not such a life as civilised people should live. (2) The chief hope of improvement lies in the development of popular government. We must extend political rights to all men, rich and poor, educated and ignorant; we must take the whole nation into counsel, and those of us who wish to govern must do so by appealing to the judgment of those who are governed. These two propositions are, as it seems to me, sound in themselves. If we wish to apply them with effect, we must lay aside illusions and abstractions, and prepare ourselves for politics by an impartial study of the facts of history and human nature.

Political Groups.

It is part of the accepted theory of English politics that there are two great homogeneous parties, one of which is in power, while the other is ready to assume the responsibilities of power if it can succeed in turning out the Government. This theory never corresponds exactly with the facts. There are always many minor parties or groups, which are important factors in every political combination. Almost any interest or opinion or craze may have its group of supporters acting together in an election, and a candidate may find himself pressed to give some modicum of recognition to a great many small parties, banded together for particular objects. Each of these is tempted to increase its own power by unreasonable insistence on its own object. Electors have been known to say, 'We think A a good politician and B a bad one, but if A does not accept our formula, we shall vote for B.' If any large number of electors were to behave in this way, it is plain that popular government would be rendered impossible.

The Uses of Party Government.

The members of a large community are never united, either in opinion or in interest. Parties and sects save society from disintegration by supplying us with forms of partial union; they bring social questions into a manageable compass by grouping similar opinions and allied interests round a limited number of central points. We might combine to promote the good of the community without distinction of party; but it is tolerably clear that we never shall. You may protest against party government, but your protest will come to nothing, unless you can form a new party to support it. In the same way, people who protest against the sectarian divisions among Christians usually end by founding a new sect, under some odd conceited name.

In the work of government, there is a constant necessity for the exercise of power; and the balance of power is constantly shifting. As between classes and parties, questions are settled, sometimes by fighting, sometimes by voting, which is a modified and civilised form of faction fighting. There is reason in voting, just as there is reason in war; but the last argument of contending bodies of men is always power. Counting heads is not a method of arriving at truth, any more than counting scalps. Citizen A is a free trader; Citizen B is a protectionist. Neither is obviously in the wrong; and if they were to argue till the end of time, neither would convince the partisans of the other. So we agree that if A can drill and bring to the poll a larger body of voters than B, he shall have the direction of our fiscal policy.

The Evils of Party Government.

If party is a necessity, it is none the less a source of many evils. It draws to itself the allegiance which we owe to the State, and it prevents us in a hundred ways from saying what is true and from doing what is right. It neutralises to a considerable extent the right of free speech. Our ablest speakers are not free to tell us exactly what they think; they are bound to pass lightly over anything which may do their party harm, and to dwell unduly on anything which may increase its credit. Again, party spirit tends to banish courtesy from political life. We are continually praising ourselves, our leaders, our principles, our public services. We deride and denounce our opponents, calling them incompetent, unpatriotic, benighted Tories, unscrupulous Radicals, and so forth. If we are in a majority, the minority is 'factious'; if we are in a minority, the majority is 'servile.' There are some who make use of these phrases without caring much about their meaning; but perhaps the most dangerous type of partisan is the man who sincerely believes what he says—the man who identifies the cause of his party with the cause of righteousness.

There is only one remedy for the evils of party government—namely, the cultivation of an impartial spirit. We must learn to acknowledge that the points on which all good citizens are agreed are more important than the points about which they differ. We must bear in mind that two men, equally honest and equally well-informed, may take entirely different views of the same set of facts. This being so, we ought not to praise ourselves because we happen to hold sound opinions; neither should we abuse our neighbours because they hold mistaken opinions.

CHAPTER X.

PRODUCTION AND EXCHANGE.

The first though not the most important object for which society exists is to provide its members with a sufficiency of food. Even in a civilised community most of the work done is done under pressure of necessity, in order to acquire that measure of wealth without which a man cannot live. If we wish to understand society, we must evidently pay special attention to the teaching of economic science, which provides us with a record of the facts relating to wealth. This science is beset with some peculiar difficulties, which ought to be noticed at the outset.

First, it deals with matters which are very complicated. The industry and trade of a civilised country present us with an immense mass of facts whose meaning and mutual connexion are often hard to trace.

Second, it deals with matters which everybody thinks he understands. The average practical man is apt to think he knows all about capital, and value, and so on, whereas in fact he has no precise ideas on such subjects, and will not take the trouble to acquire any.

Third, it deals with matters in which we all have a material interest. We live by our property or by our labour, and therefore we can hardly discuss questions relating to property and labour with scientific impartiality.

Fourth, economic science deals with problems which are also problems of morals and of law. Whether he likes it or not, the economist is constantly called on to determine what men's duties are in regard to wealth, and how far these duties ought to be defined and enforced by law.

Taking due note of these difficulties, let us resolve to be precise in our statements, and not to use any economical term unless we know exactly what it means.

Utility.

Man lives by turning to account those natural things and forces which satisfy his wants. Anything which satisfies a human want is said to be useful or to possess utility.

Economic science does not attempt to supply us with an exact standard of utility or to distinguish between natural and conventional wants. If we had a 'calculus of pleasures and pains,' economic reasoning would be more exact; but there is a personal element in such matters which defies calculation. A want which is intolerable to one man may not even be felt by another.

All men want to live and to enjoy the pleasures of life. The exceptions to this rule are too few to be worth considering.

People of low energy are satisfied with the measure of comfort to which they are accustomed. People of high energy develop new wants with every new acquisition. There is in fact no limit to their desires except such limit as, for moral reasons, they impose on themselves.

Wealth.

Some useful things cannot be enjoyed by one man to the exclusion of others. There can be no property in air or sunlight. But property can and does exist in land, money, and goods. In a free country, every man has a right of property in his own bodily and mental powers. Whatever a man holds as his property he may keep for his own use, or give away, or exchange for the property of another.

Wealth is the sum of property or exchangeable things possessed by an individual or a community.

Production and Consumption.

Wealth is produced when the form or situation of a thing is so changed as to render it useful: as when stones are built into a wall, or when the threads of flax are separated from the pulpy part of the plant and woven into linen.

In order to produce on a large scale we require, first, a large amount of power; and second, skill to direct the power so as to attain the desired result. Power is derived from human muscles, and from natural agents, such as steam and water, working under human control. Skill is of various degrees, from the manual skill of the labourer to the skill of inventors and captains of industry.

Wealth is consumed when useful things cease to be useful, as when a loaf is eaten, or when a house falls into decay. There are two modes of consumption—use and waste. Wealth is used when it serves to maintain or refine the lives of human beings, or to advance some process of production or exchange. Wealth is wasted, sometimes in mere wantonness, as when sewage is thrown into a river; sometimes in luxury, that is, in pleasures which do not refine, but enervate and degrade those who enjoy them.

Exchange.

Man can only secure material comfort by combining his efforts with those of others. Combination increases the effect of labour in two ways. First, by mere addition of strength, as when six men carry home a tree which one could not stir. Second, by division of labour and exchange of products and services.

There are two simple cases of exchange: (1) If A is a better fisher than B, and B a better gardener than A, it is plainly advantageous that each should stick to the work he does best. (2) Even if A is better at both kinds of work than B, it is advantageous that each should stick to one business, and not divide his time and attention between two.

Exchange may take place in various ways. By force, as when A makes B his slave, and compels him to do field work in return for such subsistence as A, for his own interest, chooses to allow. By custom, as when the carpenter of an Indian village community receives a fixed portion of the farmers' crop on condition of working for them whenever they require his services. By agreement, as when A and B meet in open market and get the best price they can for their respective products and services.

The direct exchange of products and services against one another is called barter or truck. This mode of exchange is attended with great disadvantages. We therefore keep one commodity, which is especially easy to measure and transfer, and we make this represent any other commodity for purposes of exchange. This representative commodity we call coin or money.

In countries where contracts are regularly enforced, any written promise or certificate of title may be used to represent products or services for purposes of exchange. A dock warrant represents goods in a particular ship or warehouse. A wages note represents services in course of being rendered on board a ship which may be thousands of miles away. A bank note represents so much coin in a vault at the bank.

Capital.

In a rude state of society men produce only what suffices for their daily wants. If they produce more, they are apt to waste the surplus in idleness or excess. But a man of progressive mind stores up the surplus, and uses it wisely. He may use it in securing himself leisure to learn and reflect. Or he may use it in assisting production by improving his tools, or by engaging in industrial processes which do not yield an immediate return.

He may also use his wealth in obtaining command of other men's labour. If A has food for two, and B has no food at all, A may employ B to make a thing, and keep him while making it, on condition that the thing when made shall belong to A. This may be a hard bargain for B, but it is a perfectly just one. Perhaps B may say, 'I made the thing, and therefore it should belong to me.' The reply to any such claim is that B did not make the thing: it was A who made it, by means of B's labour. If A had not planned to make it, B would never have had a chance of working on it at all.

When wealth is used to assist production it is called capital. The capital of a civilised community includes fixed capital—i. e. buildings, machines, and roads *used* in the course of production and exchange; and circulating capital—i. e. food, fuel, money, etc. *spent* in the course of production and exchange.

If a man has capital which he does not use himself, he may lend it to be used by somebody else. If he lends it he expects to receive it back, and also to receive some return for the advantage which the borrower obtained by using it. In fixing the rate of this return (the rate of interest, as we say) the lender considers the sacrifice he makes in not using his capital himself, and the risk he runs of losing it when he entrusts it to another. Credit is the confidence which induces people to lend capital to one another.

Much confusion has been introduced into economic arguments by the prevailing habit of using the abstract terms capital and labour to describe certain bodies of persons. Take, for instance, the popular epigram: 'It is not capital that employs labour, but labour that employs capital.' Now capital is simply wealth, and labour is simply muscular effort; neither the one nor the other can employ anything or anybody. Skilful persons employ both capital and labour in production or in exchange.

In a civilised country, almost everybody possesses either capital or credit. An English labourer has money in the bank or in his pocket, or he can get a little credit where is he known. He can therefore spend a little time in looking for work that suits him, and he can do his day's or week's work before he touches his pay.

Cost, Value, and Profit.

The cost of a thing is the sum of the sacrifices necessary to obtain it. The cost of a thing to the seller is measured by the labour and capital he spends in making it and bringing it to market. The cost of a thing to the buyer is the price he pays for it. The cost of labour to the employer is measured by his wages bill. The cost of labour to the labourer is measured by the severity and duration of his toil.

The value of a thing is the ratio in which it may be exchanged for other things. Thus, the value of a pound of tea may be indicated by saying that it is worth so many pounds of sugar. But, of course, it is most convenient to measure all values in the common standard, which is money. The value of a thing measured in money is called its price.

Some economists are accustomed to speak of 'value in use,' by which they mean utility. But this is a most unhappy phrase, which leads to hopeless confusion between exchange value (which admits of exact measurement) and utility (which, as we saw before, cannot be exactly measured). Let it be understood, then, that the value of a thing means only what it will fetch in the market.

If the price of a thing is less than its cost to the seller, the person who brought it to market has evidently made a dead loss. Every article is expected to bring a price that will replace the capital spent on it, and pay the owner for his trouble in getting it made and brought within reach of the buyer. If a manufacturer sells a thing so as to cover waste of capital, interest on borrowed capital, insurance against loss, and 'wages of supervision' to himself, the economist says he has sold at a profit. Perhaps the manufacturer would say that his notion of profit begins where the economist's definition leaves off; every seller likes to get a little more than what will pay for his cost and trouble. But the man of business and the man of science agree in thinking that there is clearly no profit on a thing unless its value exceeds its cost.

Adam Smith's language is far from exact; his theories were in some points mistaken; but the *Wealth of Nations* is still a mine of practical wisdom. Modern political economy is expounded by J. S. Mill, Cairnes, Bagehot, etc.

CHAPTER XI.

COMPETITION, MONOPOLY, RENT.

In primitive society, there is very little competition between members of the same community. Each man has his customary position, which he cannot materially improve by excelling his neighbours in industry or skill.

In civilised communities, competition enters into every department of life, and especially into industry and trade. By competition the distribution of wealth is mainly determined. Every man is pitted against his neighbours, and there are great prizes for those who succeed. There are two modes of competition, which we must endeavour to distinguish.

First, everybody is trying to carry his capital or his labour to the industry which promises to be most profitable. There is a current of men and money constantly setting towards anything which pays exceptionally well. Of course, people with fixed capital or special skill cannot join in the rush. However well cotton may be paying, you can't turn a wool-mill into a cotton-mill, or a house-painter into a mill hand, at a moment's notice. But fresh capital and fresh labour are naturally attracted to the quarter where most success is being obtained. The general result of this kind of competition is to equalise the profits made in various industries.

In the second place, all people in the same industry are underselling one another. Under the stress of competition, no producer ventures to seek a high profit on the sale of his product, lest he should be undersold and so lose his custom. Thus value is kept down near the level of cost. This is, on the whole, a benefit to society. In a civilised community, each man consumes many things, while he produces only one thing, or renders only one kind of service. He therefore gains more as consumer by low prices than he loses as producer. Things are produced in order to be consumed; therefore the consumer should be considered first, and the producer only in so far as he serves the consumer.

If there were no competition, civilised countries would be much poorer than they are. In order to produce a large aggregate of wealth, men must work hard. Taking men as we know them, we are safe in saying that there are only two motives which can be relied on to make them work—the expectation of profit and the fear of loss. Competition offers high profits to the able and strong, while it keeps the lazy and incompetent in wholesome fear of being crushed out altogether. Darwin has taught us all that competition is the natural process by which a higher type of being destroys and supersedes a lower type.

At the same time, we must admit that this great economic force works evil as well as good. Competition strengthens the self-interest of the strong, and increases the suffering of the weak. It takes all leisure out of the lives of many men, and uses up all their energies in the struggle for existence. We need not wonder, therefore, that men should speak of re-organising society in such a way as to set us free from the strain of competition. There are two ways in which this re-organisation may be effected. We may go forward to a society in which the industrial virtues will be so strong that competition will not be needed to make men work. Or we may drift back to primitive society with its narrow conservatism: we may restore the primitive system of common rights which tended to make men rely in all things on the community, in nothing on themselves. When social reformers put forward schemes by which the strain of competition would be lessened, we must examine their proposals carefully, to find out whether they do not involve an appeal to the selfishness of the weak, which is just as dangerous in its way as the selfishness of the strong.

Supply and Demand.

Any area within which goods and services are freely exchanged is called a market. Thus, we may speak of the London sugar market, or the American labour market.

In estimating the supply of any commodity in a given market we must take several circumstances into account. First, the total amount actually offered for sale. Second, the degrees of reserve with which offers are made; or, in other words, the downward limit of price at which sellers will refuse to deal, and wait for a better opportunity. And third, we must consider the facilities for increasing the supply in case of need. Sellers cannot ask a high price if they know that other goods can easily be brought into the market to compete with their own.

In estimating the demand for any commodity, we

look at the same facts from the opposite point of view. We consider how much buyers want and will pay for: what is the upward limit of price at which they will prefer to do without the thing demanded: and what are the chances of other buyers being attracted to the same market. Observe that demand is something more than desire. A poor man may desire turtle soup, but he will not think of demanding it. Demand means desire supported by purchasing power.

Supply and demand are two aspects of the same phenomenon. Commodities are supplied to a market by people who demand other commodities in exchange. And every person who demands a thing must make his demand effective by bringing his supply in his hand.

Monopoly and Speculation.

Monopoly is the right enjoyed by the owner of a commodity in general demand, of which the supply is limited. Nature limits the supply of some commodities, such as large diamonds and exquisite singing voices. The law limits the supply of others, such as copyright books and patented inventions.

Monopoly is almost always qualified by the opportunities enjoyed by intending purchasers of supplying their needs elsewhere. If a great singer charges too much, managers will prefer to employ an inferior artist. If a landlord charges too high a rent, his tenant may go to a new country where land is cheaper, or into another business where there is more chance of profit than on a highly rented farm. Monopoly is therefore temporary and qualified in its nature; but while it exists it may be made to yield large profits in skilful hands.

Speculation usually involves the attempt to obtain some advantage in the nature of a monopoly. A man lays out his money in creating a new market for a certain commodity; of this new market he has for a time exclusive command. Or he buys up land or stock or goods which he expects to be in large demand some day soon. These are all instances of speculation. I do not undertake to give any more precise definition of the term. It is indeed very difficult to draw the economical line of distinction between speculation and legitimate trade.

In our country at the present time speculation is invading every department of business. Competition makes it difficult to realise more than a small profit by safe and cautious trade. At the same time, the desire for large profits has grown stronger with the increase of the national wealth and the development of new tastes and pleasures.

Speculation does not enrich the community. At its best, it is only the concentration of many men's gains in the hands of the cleverest among them. At its worst, it is a mere gamble, from which one or two men emerge with great gains while the rest have lost everything.

It is easy to see the evils which are caused by speculation: it is not so easy to suggest a remedy. Look, for example, at the London Stock Exchange. Everybody knows that a large proportion of the business done there is merely speculative and serves no useful purpose; and Parliament has attempted to put a stop to some of the well-known practices of the place. But the attempt has failed; and the reason of the failure is this: that you cannot effectively interfere with the Stock Exchange without impairing its usefulness as an open market for all kinds of stocks and shares. A nation like ours, which owns large going concerns in all parts of the world, must have a market where investors can place and withdraw their capital with perfect facility. So long as the market exists, bold and skilful men will resort to it and take advantage of the chances which it offers.

Speculation can only be checked by increased knowledge, which will enable us to take a more accurate measure of the needs of the community and to organise production and exchange accordingly: and by improved morality, which will induce manufacturers and traders to think more of their duty to the community and less of their own immediate gain.

Property in Land.

Under the general name of land we include the soil, the minerals under it, and the capital fixed on or combined with the soil in the shape of fences, buildings, manure, etc. The value of any given piece of land is made up of three elements—the natural qualities of the soil and minerals, the amount of unexhausted capital fixed on and combined with the soil, and the advantages of the situation. Land in a settled country, near great markets, is much more valuable than land remote from civilisation. There is a great extent of good land in South America which could hardly be sold, unless at a nominal price.

We have seen that among primitive people land is held by tribal or quasi-tribal communities, who have no notion of individual property or free exchange: and how private property in land arose out of the desire of good farmers to keep their holdings long enough to secure the profits of their industry, and also out of the desire of feudal lords to make the most of their rights. When the system of private rights is established, land becomes an article of commerce. It becomes, as we may say, part of the industrial capital of the community living on it. But the land on which we live is not only our capital; it is our home; and most men would rather live moderately well at home than try the chances of a new country. This sentimental view of the land question is very important; but we must not allow sentiment to confuse our notions of economic truth. Economically speaking, there is little, if any, essential difference between property in land and property in capital. This point is so frequently misunderstood that it may be well to enumerate the reasons commonly given for making a distinction between these two kinds of property.

First, it is said that Nature made land, while man makes capital. The fact is that nature and man make both. Man takes from nature so much raw material; he compels the forces of nature to co-operate with his skill. The result is represented by settled and cultivated land, and by those other products of industry which we call capital.

Second, it is said that nature or God intended the land to be common to all who live on it. To say this of nature is absurd, for nature means only what exists: common property and private property are equally natural, for both exist. As for God's intentions, we have no right to dogmatise. God has not given us a land system; we may presume He means us to do whatever is most just and reasonable.

Third, it is said that land is the necessary basis of all industry, and therefore we ought not to allow exclusive rights to be acquired in it. This argument applies to capital just as forcibly as to land; in a civilised country one is as necessary to industry as the other. Give a labouring man ten acres of land and nothing else, and he will probably die of want. If he may claim to have the use of land because it is necessary he may claim the use of capital on the same plea.

Fourth, it is said that land is limited in quantity, whereas other kinds of wealth may be indefinitely increased. There is a measure of truth in this statement, but it is also to some extent misleading. For if you take the population of a given country at a given time, and compare their relation to land with their relation to capital, you find that the two relations are essentially alike. Capital *may* be increased, but at any given time it is a limited quantity, not more than sufficient for the needs of the people. And therefore the possession of capital involves monopoly to the same extent as the possession of land. The capitalist and the landowner both hold exclusive command of something without which the industry of their neighbours cannot be carried on.

Fifth, it is said that ownership of land enables a man to make an excessive gain without taking part in the work of the community. The value of his land increases steadily with the progress of the community:

an advantage which he shares with the owners of certain other kinds of property, as for instance bank stock. The annual return which he obtains for the use of his land is also constantly increasing: and this advantage is peculiar to land. But it must be observed that when land becomes private property it becomes also a subject of commerce. The vast majority of owners of land are purchasers and successors of purchasers who have secured the special advantages of this kind of property only by paying a high price for it. The greater number of English estates have been sold and bought once at least within the last fifty years. Each new purchaser has paid from 25 to 40 years' purchase of the rental, taking his chance of agricultural depression and other causes which may reduce the rental, taking his chance also of the profit he may make if his land is wanted for building or other industrial purposes.

On the whole, I see no *economical* reason to distinguish property in land from property in other things. Whether, and how far private property is socially useful, is a question which we shall have to consider in the next chapter.

Rent.

Rent, in the popular sense of the word, is the payment made for using land or fixed capital belonging to another. The amount of this payment is determined in various ways. By custom, as when a landlord fixes his rents at a certain rate, because his tenants have been used to pay at that rate, or because he is afraid of being boycotted if he asks more. By law, as when a special tribunal is appointed to see that landlords do not exceed the customary limit. By competition, as when a tenant offers a certain rent, knowing that the landlord can get at least as much from some other applicant. Rents are fixed by custom in places where private property in land has not been completely developed or recognised. In Ireland, for instance, a landlord is regarded not as an owner of the land, but rather as a person who collects tribute from the occupying owners. The amount of this tribute varies with the wealth and benevolence of the landlord, the prosperity of the tenants, and a variety of other causes. Rents are fixed by competition where the rights of property are clearly defined and recognised. In Scotland or in New England a man makes his bargain for a farm as he would for a cargo of wheat which he meant to sell again at a profit. The rules of commerce prevail, for good or for evil. In the slums of London, people pay high rents for very bad houses. This is not due to any difference between property in land and other property; it is due to the excessive poverty of the people, which places them at a disadvantage in making all their bargains. The same people who pay high rents for wretched lodgings pay also high prices for adulterated bread and tea.

The object of our modern laws has been to make land a subject of commerce. To say that 'all rent is an unjust and immoral tax on industry' is to display a misunderstanding of business relations. It is no more immoral to make a poor man pay for the land he requires, than to make him pay for the spade with which he tills it. Both are subjects of commerce. If the rent is exorbitant, to the knowledge of the landlord, then of course it is unjust and immoral to exact it.

CHAPTER XII.

THE DISTRIBUTION OF WEALTH.

In a well-ordered community, wealth ought to be produced in sufficient quantity, and distributed in such a way as to secure a decent average of comfort. Every person who can work ought to work; and nobody should be overworked. Every honest worker ought to have enough; and nobody ought to be exorbitantly wealthy. It must be admitted that we are still a long way from the attainment of this ideal. We produce a large aggregate of wealth, but we still have to complain of the evils caused by poverty and luxury. Before we speculate as to the causes of this state of things, we must lay down certain general principles, which form the basis of all sound political economy.

The Law of Population.

Man is an animal, and like other animals he has a tendency to multiply beyond his means of subsistence. Unlike other animals, he can emancipate himself from this tendency by exercising foresight and self-control —by taking care not to marry and produce children until he sees his way to providing for them. Unfortunately, foresight and self-control are not universal; and people who are depressed by poverty are specially tempted to be reckless in the matter of marriage and parentage. This is one reason why there are so many poor, even in wealthy countries.

The foregoing statement contains the gist of the doctrine of Malthus. It is a statement so simple and so true that in order to argue against it you must begin by missing the point, and there are able writers who miss the point in various ways. There are some who suppose Malthus to have taught that population *must* always keep ahead of subsistence. But for man there is no *must* in this matter. Marriage is a voluntary act.

Again, there are those who argue that the earth would produce plenty for all, if we only knew how to distribute wealth more evenly. But the answer to this is that men must live on the wealth which they possess, not on that which they might possess under more favourable conditions. Suppose it to be true that Ireland, rightly cultivated, could support twice her present population. How does that affect the question whether a Mayo peasant ought to marry on the prospect of succeeding to one half of a five-acre farm? Suppose it to be true that the wealth of London is unfairly absorbed by capitalists and ground landlords. How does that affect the question whether a working lad ought to marry at eighteen on 18s. a week?

Some people tell us that 'when God sends mouths, He sends food to fill them'—or would send it, if it were not intercepted by landlords, employers, and bad governments. The stern fact is, that God sends millions of mouths for which no food is provided; this is true throughout the whole animal kingdom, and it is true of man *quâ* animal. Why the fact should be so we cannot tell; it is part of the mystery of pain and evil, which baffles human understanding. But the fact itself is clear enough for all practical purposes.

Self-interest and Independence.

In order to produce the wealth required by a civilised community, a great deal of hard and disagreeable work must be done. There are some men who work hard because they love their work, or because they desire to be useful to their neighbours. But these men are exceptional; the average man does not work hard unless he is stimulated by the hope of profit or by the fear of want. If therefore you deprive men altogether of the hope of profit or relieve them altogether of the fear of want, production will be checked and the general level of comfort will be lowered.

This is the economic doctrine of self-interest, of which so many hard things have been said. Economists are often charged with advocating self-interest as a principle; it would be more accurate to say that they assert it as a fact. Perhaps economists are not sufficiently careful to point out that self-interest, however indispensable it may be, always contains an element of danger. There are many men in whom the hope of profit has been sharpened into greed; there are many on whom the fear of want weighs continually, making them slaves to appetite and necessity. While we recognise self-interest as a fact, we recognise it as one of the facts which ought to be altered.

In the mind of a good citizen, self-interest takes that higher form which we call the sentiment of independence. A man may well be forward in seeking work and careful in looking after his pay, if he wishes to live honestly, without being too much beholden either to the community or to his friends.

Property.

The existing distribution of wealth is based on private property and free contract. We must therefore examine these principles before going further.

Any private person may own goods or land to an indefinite amount; and an owner cannot be compelled to give or lend what he owns, except on terms agreeable to himself. This rule is maintained partly because it satisfies our instinctive love of property. Every man likes to keep what he has, and even those who have nothing look forward to doing as they like with their own, when they get it. But private property is protected by law for other reasons. It answers several important social purposes.

In the first place, it affords a sound basis for family independence. A man who owns money or land is in a position to place his wife and children beyond the danger of want. Without property, the family would lose half its significance, and the family is the moral unit of a well-ordered society. It is so because it supplies the ordinary man with an unselfish motive for doing his duty. Few men are capable of working hard for a merely philanthropic purpose; but we are almost all willing to work for those who have natural claims upon us.

Again, there are many operations connected with the management of land and capital, which are most efficiently performed by private persons, working at their own risk and for their own advantage. In ancient times, when land was cultivated in common, under strict customary rules, it was cultivated badly; and we have seen that private property came in partly because the good farmer did not like to see his allotment pass into other hands. If we should now revert to the system of common rights, we could not fall back on customary rules; we should have to adopt political rules, laid down by the State and enforced by its officials. Now it is a matter of common knowledge that officials are less active, less frugal, and less eager for improvement than private traders. If a trader cannot keep down expenses, and find out what people want to buy, he appears in the *Gazette*. But a Secretary of State may keep fifty unnecessary clerks, and send out stores to all the places where they are not wanted, without any risk of appearing in the *Gazette*, unless perhaps when he is raised to the peerage. Some people speak of the State as if it could do anything; but there are some simple operations which the State is almost incapable of performing. Take a few examples.

1. Saving and investment of capital. There is a great consumption of capital constantly going on, and this loss is repaired by the action of individuals, who put by part of their income in the hope of investing it so as to yield a return. If rent and interest were suppressed, saving would be checked, and the State would have to levy and put by a part of the common income to provide for repairs of fixed capital, &c. But the State finds it almost impossible to save; and popular governments especially have much difficulty in making both ends meet. There are many pressing needs which a government has to provide for; as soon as it has

money in hand, it is called upon to start some new scheme, to pay off some war charges or other extraordinary debt, or to relieve its subjects by reducing taxation. Government therefore cannot well be trusted with the enormous capital required for the industry of a civilised nation.

2. *Invention and experiment.* The improvements from which we derive material benefit are often the result of a great sacrifice of time and capital. If a man wishes to develope a new machine or a new process, he must use his own property or persuade others to lend their property for the purpose; and this is a great security against reckless projects. But if the State attempted industrial experiments, it would do so in the official way, drawing on the Treasury to make good all its failures, and pursuing its schemes long after they had ceased to pay.

3. *Valuation.* At present each man obtains for his special product or service just what others are willing to give for it; and this simple rule solves an infinite number of problems. But free sale and purchase imply that the things sold and the prices given for them are the property of those who sell and buy. Without property it is hard to see how the complicated exchanges of civilised life could be carried on. There are those who think that we could do without property if each man would work according to his powers, and enjoy according to his wants. That would be a good formula to apply in a community of men all willing to work hard, and all willing to consume only what they need. But I do not know any actual community which corresponds to this description.

H

Freedom of Contract.

It is part of the policy of our law that men should be free to make their own bargains. When they do so, they must fulfil their mutual promises, or pay the penalty for breach of contract. To this general rule there are exceptions of some importance.

First, there are contracts which the law will not enforce. If A promises to lend money to B for the purpose of bribing voters, this is plainly not a promise to be enforced at the suit of B.

Again, there are persons whom the law regards with special tenderness, by reason of their inability to protect themselves. If a person under 21, for example, enters into a contract with a person of full age, the 'infant' may enforce the contract, but the other party may not.

Modern legislation has extended the same privilege to certain classes of persons who have been found unable to protect themselves against oppression. The Employers Liability Act, for instance, proceeds on the assumption that workmen cannot secure satisfactory conditions of service without the help of the State. The Irish Land Acts were rendered necessary, as their authors declared, by the 'incapacity of the Irish tenant to contract with his landlord.' Acts of this kind have done good; but the benefits which they confer are of a qualified sort. They tend to impair the self-reliance of the persons protected; and they do not always promote a good understanding between the classes concerned. The Irish Land Acts have removed some old abuses, but they have not brought contending interests closer together. Landlords and tenants have learned to meet one another, not as parties to a business transaction, but as litigants and political opponents, whose quarrels must be decided by the expensive methods of Courts and Parliaments.

'Necessity.'

Wherever private property exists, those who own it are liable to the censure of their poorer neighbours, and of politicians who claim to speak for the poor. The reason of this is, that property enables its owners to make a profit out of the necessities of their neighbours. If owners take a harsh advantage of their rights, they do wrong. But we cannot lay it down for a social law that no such advantage is to be taken. If on the plea of necessity a man may claim to have land or food or a loan of capital on easier terms than free contract would permit, such claims would soon multiply so as to eat up all the wealth of owners.

The necessities of which we speak are not inevitable necessities; they are created by the acts of human beings. Look, for instance, at the way in which a necessitous population is sometimes created in England. A sudden demand arises for the goods made in a particular town. At once capitalists rush into new ventures; working people leave their situations elsewhere and flock in, attracted by the prospect of high wages; so long as high wages last, working lads and girls are encouraged to marry early. When the period of prosperity passes away, the smaller capitalists are all in difficulties, and there is a crowd of working people out of work and badly off. These evils have been brought about by the eagerness of capitalists to make money and by the eagerness of working people to enjoy high wages. Unless you can make both classes more patient and prudent, you cannot produce much effect by altering the laws of property. Suppose the industry of such a town as I have described were placed under a Board, to be managed for the general good: would the social problem be solved? Most probably not. The greedy capitalist might get himself elected to the Board, and find some way of making an underhand fortune, as members of revolutionary Boards have often done. The short-sighted workman would vote for those members of the Board who promised the largest immediate dividend. So long as large dividends were paid there would be a great many early marriages, and people would bring in their friends and relations to share in the prosperity of the town. And then if the Board had a few bad years, the social problem would recur in an aggravated form.

The advantage of our system of property and free contract is this, that it makes men responsible for their necessities. Each man is bound to find some work which he can do, and for which somebody is willing to pay him. This is a stern rule; but the man who can live under it is more of a man than if his work were found for him, and his reward doled out by some superior power.

Those who wish to break down the rights of property on the plea of necessity are often led into mistakes because they pay exclusive attention to the large owners. It seems hard that one man should be without the means of living while his neighbour has far more land or capital than he needs. But when we speak of property generally we must remember that the great majority of owners are not rich, but only more or less well-to-do. The small owners, not the large owners, are the most efficient protectors of property. If a working man becomes the owner of a freehold cottage which he does not wish to occupy, he will not see any justice in a law for reducing or confiscating rent. Or if he has savings to invest he will not be attracted by a State Bank which says, 'We shall be happy to take your money, and we will lend it to a virtuous Irishman who is going to start in life as a peasant farmer. When you require your capital, we hope to be able to pay it out to you. But you will not get any interest, because there is a new law which says that usury is wrong.'

How Wealth is Distributed.

If you make out a scheme showing how the income of a great community is distributed, you will find that the incomes enjoyed by individuals may be classified under three heads :—(1) Rent and interest—payments for the use of property. (2) Salaries, fees, and wages—payments for services rendered. (3) Profits of exchange and speculation.

Rent.

Rent is a payment made to the owners of land and fixed capital for leave to occupy and use it. The amount of this payment is fixed, as we have seen, chiefly by competition. The total amount of rent paid in a civilised country increases with the prosperity of the country. Thus, 200 years ago this nation was paying ten millions sterling to the owners of land; now we are paying sixty millions. But as industry becomes more various and more skilful, income from other sources increases more rapidly than rent; and rent forms a smaller proportion of the whole. Thus, 200 years ago, rent stood for a fourth of the national income; now it stands for less than a twentieth.

The persons who receive and have an interest in rent belong to various classes. There are the landowners, great and small, and there are also many persons who enjoy incomes charged on land, and who have invested capital on the security of land. In some cases rent is divided and to some extent disguised by special arrangements. Thus the rent of an Irish farm usually includes, (1) The rent payable to the landlord in respect of his property in the land, and (2) Interest on the capital sum paid to the outgoing tenant in respect of *his* property in the land.

What benefit does the community receive in return for rent? This question has been partly answered above under the general heading 'Property.' Large owners of land are usually expected to pay particular attention to their public duties. There are some, indeed, who devote themselves entirely to sport and other forms of amusement; there are others who devote themselves with praiseworthy diligence to the details of local government. Our unpaid magistrates, for instance, are open to criticism; but they are probably more efficient and less expensive than small salaried officials would be.

Interest.

Interest is a payment for the use of capital. The rate of interest depends on various circumstances. If the lender runs a risk of losing his capital, he adds something by way of insurance against the risk : this is one reason why poor people have to pay high interest when they borrow. If the capital seeking borrowers is large, and the openings for employing it are comparatively few, the rate of interest will fall. It follows that in old wealthy countries, where capital is plentiful and security good, the rate of interest is low. But although the *rate* may fall, capital accumulates so rapidly, and is lent so readily, that the *total amount* of interest paid is constantly increasing.

For the benefit which the community receives in return for interest paid, I must refer again to the general heading 'Property.' As for the people who receive interest, they are of every class, from the great financiers who lend only great sums, down to the small people who save and invest small sums.

Salaries and Fees.

Rent and interest are, as we have seen, payments for the use of property. Payments for services rendered may be classified according to the nature of the work done. Those who render services of an intellectual or administrative nature are paid by yearly salary, or by fees. We all know, in a general way, how the rate of these payments is fixed. If a bank manager is wanted, we look for a man of suitable education and training, able to hold his own in the upper rank of commercial society; and his salary is fixed according to the standard of living in his own class. If we consult a physician, we pay him the fee required by the rules of his profession. If a man has a great reputation for skill, or if his duties are very important, he will expect his salary or his fees to yield him a large income.

In civilised countries, the number of professional persons and salaried officials usually bears an unduly large proportion to the total population, and the proportion tends to increase. Our philanthropic movements, for example, and our experiments in popular legislation, almost always result in the creation of new places; and the spread of education swells the number of young men who look out for places, or try the chances of the professions.

Wages.

The majority of bread-winners in this country live by wages which are paid to them fortnightly, weekly, or at shorter intervals, by their employers.

The *total amount* of employment given and wages paid varies according to the amount of capital seeking investment, and according to the opportunities which exist for investing it, so as to obtain a good rate of interest and profit.

The *rate* of wages, or in other words the exchange-value of labour, depends on a number of causes, which must be separately considered.

First, it depends on the number of persons seeking employment. Where labourers are few, in proportion to the work to be done, employers will have to pay high wages. In old countries, the labour-market is kept full and over-full by the growth of population, and wages are forced down by competition.

Second: the rate of wages varies according to the

efficiency of the labourer. Strong, diligent, skilful men are worth much to their employer; they know their worth, and he knows it, and they must be well paid. Here it may be well to note that 'cheap labour,' in the employer's sense of the phrase, ought not to mean underpaid labour. If, for instance, a contractor has to make a railway in Italy, it pays him to employ Englishmen at high wages rather than Italians whom he can get at half the price. Working men, therefore, have an interest in improving the efficiency of their labour. If they are tempted to give their employer as little as they can for his money, they should remember that every rule or custom which makes their labour less valuable tends in the long run to lower their wages.

Third: the rate of wages depends not only on the labourer's efficiency in his work, but on his habits and standard of living. If men are used to good food, nice houses, and other comforts, they will put themselves in the way of having them; they will develope their independence and their power of combination so as to take up a stronger position towards their employers. In the last fifty years, there has been a marked improvement in the tastes of labouring people; and this improvement has helped to secure for the labourers a considerable share of the wealth yielded by modern methods of production. Unhappily, there are always some labourers whose standard of living is low. They are content with a dirty, careless style of housekeeping, and they are content that their children should be like themselves. If they have a rise of wages, they live much as before, and drink or gamble away part of their earnings. Men of this stamp sometimes say that they are nobody's enemies but their own. They are in truth the enemies of every working man; they lower the status and retard the prosperity of the whole labouring class.

Fourth: the rate of wages depends to some extent on the state of society generally. If labour is despised, as it is among slave-holding nations, the labourers will be depressed. If labour is admitted to social equality, there will be a disposition to treat the labourer, as we treat a tradesman or a salaried officer in whom we may happen to take a friendly interest. Observe that policy as well as friendly feeling should lead us to treat the labourer well; for good treatment (provided it is not administered in such a way as to impair independence) raises the personal worth of a man, and increases the efficiency of his work.

Is the sum distributed in wages a fair return for the services rendered? This is an extremely difficult question, and we must beware of accepting the off-hand answers commonly given to it. Some say that wages must be fair because they are fixed by free contract. But where there is property on one side and necessity on the other, free contract is not always fair. There are cases where the law says, and indeed must say, 'This is a contract; the parties must carry it out'—where the moral judgment says, 'The contract may be legal, but it is not fair.'

Again, there are those who argue that wages are always or almost always unfair. They tell us that wealth is produced by labour—therefore, they say, all the wealth of a country belongs of right to the labourers. This argument proceeds on a total misconception of what is meant by production. Wherever there is free exchange, production means making and offering for use or sale something which people want, and are ready to pay for. The producer is he who studies the wants and the purchasing power of the community, and undertakes to supply them. In our large industries, these functions are not usually performed by the labourers. The navvies who work on a railway do not produce it; they render a mechanical service, for which they are paid, whether the line succeeds or not. The railway is produced by the men who find out that it is wanted, and who undertake to construct a line that can be worked at a profit in competition with other lines. If their enterprise succeeds, it is hard to see how the navvies can claim a share in the profits.

The weak point in the modern wage-earner's position is just this, that he is not a producer, but a mechanical agent in the work of production. Co-operative undertakings aim at improving the position of the labourers by enabling them to perform the functions which are usually performed by capitalists and contractors, and so to become receivers of interest and profits as well as of wages.

Profits.

In a previous chapter I defined profit as the amount by which the value of a thing exceeds its cost. The cost of an article to a master-manufacturer includes many items—price of materials and fuel, wear and tear of plant, interest on capital, rent and wages. The cost of an article to a trader includes the price he pays for it, and the expenses incurred in offering it for sale. Every manufacturer and trader would like to obtain a price sufficient to cover the cost of his article, and to leave him a large margin of profit. But he has to face many competitors, all anxious to undersell him, and he is driven to cut his profit finer and finer. Where competition is keen, it is not possible to make a large sum by profits in the ordinary course of trade.

To make large profits in these times, a man must have exceptional enterprise, ability, or luck. He may carry his goods to some new market, in Central Africa or elsewhere. He may buy up and develope some new invention. He may buy and sell on speculation, trusting to his cleverness or his luck to come out a winner. Lastly, he may do business on a very large scale, so that a low rate of profit will yield him a good aggregate return. It is in order to obtain a very large business that modern traders advertise, and make 'rings' and 'corners,' and sink capital in underselling and ruining their rivals.

It is by no means easy to answer the question, What is a fair profit? I venture to suggest that profits are fair when they yield the trader a proper remuneration for the service which he renders to the community. Thus, for example, a man who keeps a large well-conducted shop, where many people find what they want, may be taken to deserve an income equal to that of a Bank manager or a moderately high official. The profit on each transaction should represent the service which he does for his customer by keeping the article for sale.

Does the total sum distributed in profits amount to

more than a fair return for the useful work done by traders and financiers ? This is another of the difficult questions to which offhand answers are given with easy confidence. There are those who assert that open competition produces, in trade as in other departments of life, an accurate distribution of rewards according to merit. In the face of the undoubted evils wrought by speculation and commercial rivalry, this position cannot be maintained. Others again denounce 'profit-mongers' as a class, overlooking the fact that traders are necessary to the free exchange of products between man and man, town and town, nation and nation. The average income of traders is probably not larger than we should have to pay to our buying and selling agents if exchange were organized on some co-operative plan. If the evils of the profit-system are to be abated, we must apply ourselves to the extension of co-operative methods, by which reward may be distributed according to merit, and all forms of speculative trading discouraged. We must also endeavour to cultivate true social opinions about wealth and its possessors. As things now stand, a man who makes a large fortune becomes a social and political power, whatever his character may be; and the love of power combines with the love of pleasure to stimulate the feverish anxiety of traders to be rich.

For the subjects treated in this chapter, see the works on political economy before referred to. Ricardo's theory of rent and wages is now admitted to depend on assumptions of doubtful validity: it has furnished a basis for the socialist reasoning of Karl Marx and Henry George.

CHAPTER XIII.

SOCIAL INEQUALITIES.

AMONG civilised men, labour and wealth are very unequally distributed. We see a few families enjoying great wealth for which they are not obliged to work, and a large number of families working hard for mere subsistence. We also see many families, some of them just as virtuous as their wealthy neighbours, who struggle along as they can, and never have enough. It is natural that this state of things should produce a resentful feeling in many minds. But we cannot reason carefully under the influence of resentment. We must, therefore, lay aside all emotion—even sympathetic emotion—and look quietly at the facts before we venture to propose a remedy for the evils of Society.

It seems to me that the inequalities of which we complain are due to the long-continued operation of various causes, some of which I shall attempt to enumerate.

1. *Personal Inequality.*—A strong and clever man will always be able to secure a larger share of wealth and power than his neighbours. If he is also a selfish man, it will be difficult to prevent him from acquiring an exorbitant share. And even if he is not selfish he may act in a selfish way simply because he has never learned his social duty. Almost every rich man has a hazy, but perfectly sincere notion that he benefits the community by adding to his own wealth, and by living in

what he considers a suitable style. Almost every man who wields power comes to think that the general interest would be promoted if his fellow-citizens would only submit to his ascendancy.

2. *Political Inequality.*—Apart from personal differences, there are distinctions of rank, without which no society has ever succeeded in keeping order and holding its own. Above the mass of men who work and fight there must be officers to command; and above them, again, there are the persons in whom the powers of the State are vested. Those who exercise high authority are almost always able to insist on a reward in proportion to their dignity. This holds true of governing persons who derive their authority from the people, as well as of those who profess to govern by rights which are independent of the people.

3. *Social Inequality.*—Every family has a certain regard to its 'position in society,' and arranges its habits accordingly. Hence the division of modern communities into classes.

Each class has a code of its own, which is enforced by social pressure. Thus, for example, a man of the middle class must come up to a certain standard of manners: he must live and dress in a certain way, and possess a certain amount of money. If he falls below the mark in any of these respects, no girl of his class will be allowed to marry him, and he may, perhaps, be 'turned out of society.' In the same way, the aristocracy have their standard, and the well-to do section of the labouring people have theirs. Unhappily, each class is tempted to keep up its standard by seeking the familiar intercourse of the class above it, and by avoiding familiar intercourse with the class below it. The lines of separation thus drawn are rendered dangerously distinct by the habits of great cities, in which different classes usually occupy different streets and quarters.

Inequality is eminently natural—so natural that no change in our institutions would enable us to reduce men to equality. Some men are born to govern, and some to obey: some to make money, and some to muddle it away. But if inequality is natural, it does not follow that the glaring contrasts presented by modern society are necessary or desirable. It is not good that some men should be very rich; neither is it good that many men should be very poor. We ought, therefore, to favour such social agencies as make for a more even distribution of wealth, comfort, and refinement.

Revolution and Reform.

Some politicians have brooded over the inequalities of society until they have come to desire a Revolution—a great uprising against tyranny and injustice. When the Revolution has been safely accomplished, they hope to see society take a fresh start, and a better state of things inaugurated. Such hopes have often been cherished before, and they have always been disappointed.

You cannot make a Revolution unless you persuade a large number of people that they may, if they choose, effect a great and immediate change for the better in their own condition. And when men have made a Revolution, they always discover that it is simply impossible to effect a great and immediate change for the better in the condition of a large number of human beings. Hence arise disappointments, recriminations, and active disorder; until at last the victims of Revolution fall into a hopeless mood, and cling to any 'Saviour of Society' who will undertake to restore a semblance of the old order.

The cardinal error of Revolutionary politicians is this, that they assume the possibility of breaking away from custom and tradition. They look on institutions as if they were purely artificial, and therefore alterable at pleasure. In point of fact, institutions are rooted in the natures of the men who are accustomed to them. If all our laws were destroyed in a day, our habits and ways of thinking would remain, and out of these a new set of laws, not very unlike the old, would soon be developed. If we desire great changes, we must not put our trust in Revolution; we must work steadily at those reforms which seem most likely to improve our habits and ways of thinking. The reforms which tend most effectually to redress inequalities are those which tend to the diffusion of property and power. We may promote their diffusion in two ways—by preventing their undue concentration in the hands of the few, and by rendering acquisition and independent action more easy for the mass of mankind.

The Diffusion of Property.

Measures for the diffusion of property may be summarised as follows:—

1. We may prevent the concentration of property by weakening the motives which impel men to accumulate more than enough. We do this, in the first place,

by discouraging luxury and idleness. If rich men were expected to work, and to live simply, they would find themselves as well off with a moderate fortune as with an excessive one. Under this head there is not much to be effected by compulsion of law. Sumptuary laws have always done more harm than good, and they involve an unpleasant amount of interference with family life. Laws for compelling the rich to work could not safely be administered by any ordinary government. The country would not gain much by empowering a stupid inspector to send Darwin into a factory and Tennyson into a counting-house.

2. We may prevent the concentration of property by limiting the power of settlement. Our law has always discouraged 'Perpetuities'—that is, arrangements for keeping property tied up through several generations. Within certain limits, the power of settlement is useful; it is fair enough, for instance, that a man should leave the income of his property to his widow, and the property itself to his children after her. But the power of settlement has often been used to keep a large estate together, in the hands of one person; and all such arrangements should be discouraged. The rule of law which gives the whole of a man's landed property, not disposed of by will, to his eldest son, is open to grave objection, and ought to be altered.

There are some proposals in regard to property which go further still. Thus, it is proposed to deprive owners of property of the right to make a will; the State is invited to appropriate the property of deceased owners, except what is necessary to provide for their children. A law of this kind would lead to confusion by tempting every owner to make gifts of his property in his lifetime, retaining the income for himself. It would also work great hardship if applied to small owners, and great injustice if an arbitrary line were drawn between large owners and small.

Again, it is proposed to make the rich pay ransom for being rich, by means of graduated taxation. It is right that public burdens should be graduated according to ability to pay : but it may be doubted whether taxation is a fit instrument for correcting inequalities of fortune. Suppose a heavy ransom had to be paid on accumulations over a certain amount. Every owner over that amount would be tempted to conceal his wealth by dividing it—by holding portions of it in the names of others. Such secret arrangements have often been made to defeat strict laws ; and they do considerable mischief, because they tend to discredit the law, and also because inquisitorial measures have to be taken to check them.

3. Acquisition is rendered easy to the mass of men by all measures which encourage thrift. Savings Banks, Friendly Societies, and Building Societies have done much for this nation, and they may do yet more. There are those who would like to see all our land and capital handed over to the State or to Local Boards. We shall avoid the necessity of trying any such experiment if we can enable every head of a family to become a capitalist and a landowner.

4. Acquisition is also rendered easy by making the transfer of property as simple and cheap as possible. One cause of the undue concentration of property, and especially of land, may be found in the obscurity of our law and the cost of legal forms. These obstacles to the acquisition of small properties ought to be removed.

In some cases the law has gone so far as to assist persons who wish to acquire small properties, by enabling them to draw on the resources and the credit of the State. Thus, for instance, an Irish peasant who wishes to buy his holding can obtain an advance of money from the State on easier terms than he could get it by private bargain. Such laws may be justified by special necessities, but they have to be carefully watched. If the State puts a man in possession of property, he is rather apt to look to the State to help him if he cannot manage to make a profit out of it; and so in various ways he is tempted to act imprudently. It is well known that the Irish peasants borrowed money too readily on the strength of the rights given them by the Land Act of 1870, and this was one reason why the State had to give them a further measure of assistance in 1881.

The Diffusion of Power.

The distribution of power in a community must correspond, more or less, to the distribution of property; but property alone cannot confer independence or influence. Again, the distribution of power is, in a measure, determined by political laws, but a man may have political rights without having any influence on affairs. If you wish to have power you must have character—you must have a steadfast purpose, and a clear perception of the means by which your purpose can be effected.

If we wish to see power more generally diffused, we must increase the number of clear-headed and public-spirited individuals.

There are two kinds of power which we desire to

see more generally diffused, with a view to the correction of Social Inequalities :—

1. Industrial and financial power. Labouring men have often very little notion of the complex arrangements which are necessary to the success of the industries in which they are engaged; they do not look beyond their own work, and therefore they are dependent on the few who know how to manage great undertakings. If the labourers wish to be more independent of the managing men, they must acquire the power of management. This will be a difficult process, but the industrial problem cannot be solved in any other way. State Socialism is not a solution, for the State cannot teach men the art of management. It can remove the managing capitalist, and put the managing official in his place, but we cannot be sure that the labouring man would gain by the change.

2. Political power. The ordinary citizen often knows very little of the mechanism of government, and therefore he is too much at the mercy of officials and professional politicians. The mere possession of a vote does not imply the possession of political power. If we desire to be independent, we must increase the number of individuals who exercise an independent judgment on public affairs. Party managers must be made to feel that they cannot count on our votes unless their acts are in accordance with the principles to which we adhere.

The argument for and against revolutionary methods is best illustrated in the recent history of France. See Bryce's *American Commonwealth* for the description of a community in which a kind of equality subsists, in spite of great inequality in the distribution of wealth and power.

CHAPTER XIV.

THE FUNCTIONS OF THE STATE.

The agencies for good which are at work in a civilised community may be thus classified : (1) voluntary agencies set in motion by the hope of profit; (2) voluntary agencies set in motion by public spirit and the desire to do good ; (3) the State, which acts by compulsion. In a free country the State does not act without the previous consent of a considerable number of its subjects; but when that consent is obtained, the purpose of the State is carried out by force of law. Money required for State purposes is obtained by means of taxation; and this power of taking money by force tends to swell the cost of all operations undertaken by the State.

Being entrusted with power to make and enforce laws, the State is often tempted to push its activity too far. All public authorities have to be watched, lest they should encroach on individual and family independence. Government and legislation can do much for us, but they cannot do everything; nor can they do anything without aid from other powers. Even the business of national defence will not be well done by the State, unless there are other agencies at work, supplying the State with hardy, loyal citizens.

We shall now consider separately the various functions performed by the modern State for its subjects.

National Defence.

The States of Christendom are accustomed to settle disputed questions by war. Before this custom can be altered, a very great change must take place in our ideas and habits. In the mean time, every State must be prepared to defend its territory and the inhabitants thereof against all enemies from without. Resistance to aggression is perfectly in accordance with the highest morality. A good man forgives those who trespass against him; but he also co-operates in putting a stop to trespassing. If the men of England were to sit still and allow their wives and children to be carried into slavery by a French army, they would be acting not like Christians but like cowards. If an English Minister were to give up any interest committed to his care out of mere dislike to war, he would be acting not morally but pusillanimously. We ought to be willing to fight on a just occasion; and if we are willing we must also be ready.

There are two ways in which the State may make provision for national defence.

1. Every able-bodied citizen may be required to submit to military training, and to serve the country in case of necessity. This plan is followed with great success in Germany, where the State can place all the best of its male subjects in the field on a short notice. The burden of such a system is indeed enormous. Many strong hands are withdrawn from industry by the compulsory training; many young men emigrate rather than enter the army; and the maintenance of so large a force tends to perpetuate despotic government. At the same time, it is hard to see how any

continental nation can dispense with a large army. States are so unscrupulous in taking advantage of one another that no nation can disarm unless other nations agree to do the same, and it is almost impossible to believe that any such agreement would be loyally carried out.

2. The State may hire soldiers to defend the general body of its subjects. If the persons hired are foreigners, they are called mercenaries. There are strong political objections to mercenary armies. Experience has shown that they may be used by a despotic government to coerce its own native subjects. Even when hired soldiers are citizens of the State which employs them (as in our own country) the system is open to grave objection. Military life cannot be made attractive to the average respectable young man; and therefore professional armies are composed in large measure of young men who have not attained a respectable position. There is great difficulty in making up the required number of men; and each soldier costs the country a large sum of money. It is usually said that we retain our system of voluntary enlistment because the British labouring classes would not stand the introduction of compulsory service.

We cannot provide for the necessities of war without throwing a heavy burden on the industrious community. It is the part of a good citizen to bear his share of the burden, and to fight if the defence of the country requires it. Our volunteer service enables the citizen to qualify himself for this public duty; and if this service is actively developed, it may save us from danger if some continental despot should attempt to follow in the track of Napoleon.

Foreign Affairs.

The State not only provides for national defence, but it also represents us in all our relations with other States. In this department of politics a large discretion is given to the Executive. The Queen and her Ministers may bind us to any extent by treaties; they may even declare war and make peace without consulting Parliament. Even if we were to make a rule that treaties should be ratified by Parliament, or that war should not be declared without its consent, it is plain that the government must always have the real guidance of foreign affairs in its own hands. Suppose, for instance, we have to make an arrangement with Russia about the frontier of Afghanistan. The arrangement is made after some haggling between our Foreign Minister and the Russian authorities. Our Minister, if he is to negotiate with success, must have power to make concessions to the other side; he must also have power to say 'If you do not accept this or that condition, we shall go to war.'

These powers are so important that Ministers are specially bound to be explicit in stating the objects of their foreign policy. As a general rule, Ministers are not explicit. They know that the public has but little detailed knowledge of foreign affairs, and therefore they put us off with vague assurances.

The traditions of diplomacy are all in favour of secrecy. When our Government is engaged in negotiations, we are always told that it is not for the public interest to reveal what is going on, until the negotiations are over. This way of conducting foreign affairs is well suited to a State like Russia, where the government is absolute; it is not very well suited to a country like our own, where the government is subject to criticism.

Repression of Crime.

As the State protects us against enemies from without, it protects us also against enemies within. Any person who injures his neighbour by force or fraud is treated as an enemy of society. The measures taken against such enemies fall under several heads.

1. Prevention. The State provides policemen to watch over us by night and day. It lays hold of persons who are about to commit crimes; it also lays hold of young persons likely to become habitual offenders, and sends them to Reformatories.

2. Detection. The State directs inquiry in all cases where there is reason to believe that a crime has been committed. This inquiry may be open or secret; for the State employs agents who use disguise and deception in order to obtain information about criminals; and it encourages criminals to inform on one another. Whether these practices are justifiable, is a nice question of political casuistry.

3. Prosecution. If a crime is committed, the persons injured or their friends will usually endeavour to set the law in motion against the wrong doer. But we cannot trust entirely to private prosecutors; in the interest of the community, public officers are bound to see that every reasonably suspected person is brought to trial.

4. **Punishment.** When an offender is tried and found guilty, the State assigns his punishment. In doing so, various considerations must be kept in view. The wrong done must be redressed, as far as possible, by depriving the criminal of the profits of his crime, and (in some cases) by compensating the person injured. Again, the punishment must be such as to deter others from committing the same offence; the more heinous the offence, the more powerful the deterrent must be made.

The amendment of the criminal can hardly be considered one of the direct objects of his punishment; but it is not left out of sight. Convicts are compelled to go to chapel; and they are usually taught a trade. Another incidental consideration is, that a convict should not be made too burdensome to the community. His labour should be turned to profitable account; and his food, etc., should be on a very frugal scale.

Political Crimes.

Crimes committed in carrying on civil war, open insurrection, and political agitation are and must be punished by the government which is attacked. But when order has been restored, it is often wise to include political offenders in a general act of amnesty; and when such offenders escape to a foreign country, they are not usually surrendered to their own government like ordinary criminals. The question, whether it is right to treat a particular class of political offenders with exceptional levity, is a question of policy, to be decided according to circumstances, and not according to general rules.

Offences are not political merely because they are committed with a political motive. No special indulgence is due to persons who combine to injure and annoy an individual, because he is out of sympathy with them and their opinions.

Every act of indulgence is an exercise of political discretion; not a judicial act. Suppose, for example, that an honest, hot-headed man has broken the law, because he has a confused notion that the law is unjust. The judges and officials who have to deal with him must not make any difference between such a man and any other law-breaker; the essence of criminal justice is, that it should be the same for everybody. The supreme political powers may remit or reduce his punishment, if they choose to take the responsibility of relaxing the general rules of law in his favour.

Civil Justice.

Men have always been disposed to quarrel; and they cannot safely be left to settle their differences among themselves. To prevent oppression and disorder, the State steps in to administer justice. It lays down general rules, which everybody must obey, and it provides courts of law for settling disputes as they arise.

The courts are constantly at work deciding questions of right. If A claims property which is in possession of B, he brings an action; if he succeeds, the court will lend him the force of the State, if necessary, to recover his property. If A claims to be the wife of B, who refuses to recognise her, a court will inquire into the case; if she makes out her case, B will be compelled to receive and maintain her.

The Limits of the State.

There are many able men who think that the State should confine itself to the work of maintaining peace and order, leaving the material and moral welfare of the community to be promoted by voluntary effort. This opinion does not guide the course of practical politics to any great extent; all governments, popular and despotic, are more disposed to encroach than to retire. The State has given up some functions which it once exercised, but, on the other hand, it interferes with many matters which it formerly left alone. There is hardly any interest or pursuit which is not brought within the scope of modern politics.

Religion.

In early times nobody doubted that the State ought to have a religion, and to impose that religion on all its subjects. England, for example, was once a Catholic country, and none could enjoy the rights of an Englishman unless he was a Catholic. A heretic or an atheist was a kind of outlaw. Toleration has entirely altered the old state of things. In England to-day an atheist is free to buy and sell, to marry and bring up children, to spread his opinions by speech and writing, and to serve any public office, with very few exceptions. It is therefore no longer correct to speak of England as a Christian State in the sense which was attached to the phrase in the 17th century.

Nobody now supposes that the State can compel its subjects to be religious; but most Englishmen think that it should use its influence in favour of religion. We cannot include the nation in one Church, but there is a strong body of opinion in favour of maintaining the historically national Church, endowed with property devoted to religious uses at a time when the Church was identical with the nation. This arrangement is usually defended chiefly if not wholly on grounds of expediency. It is contended that the endowments and privileges of the Church make it more powerful as an agency for good among the people.

On the other hand, many Liberal politicians contend that the balance of justice and expediency inclines towards the general adoption of the voluntary principle. They argue that if the State tolerates the existence of several Churches in one nation, all Churches must be treated alike; no one must be favoured socially or politically. They disclaim hostility to the established Church as a religious body, and they hold that the Church would be more powerful for good if it were deprived of its privileges and endowments, and compelled to rely on the voluntary efforts of its own members. They do not, for the most part, aim at separating religion from politics; they wish to see politics purified and elevated by the influence of religious men; but they deny that the State has any religious function.

Science.

There are some ways in which the State can help to advance scientific inquiry without going beyond its ordinary functions. Thus, for example, the Admiralty can direct its officers to collect facts which are of great value to geographers and biologists; the Board of Trade can place its statistics at the command of the economists, and the keepers of public records can assist the researches of historians and jurists. But this indirect assistance does not satisfy the demands made by some scientific men. Like the teachers of religion, the teachers of science claim to be endowed out of public funds.

Is it really one of the functions of the State to give direct pecuniary encouragement to research? In considering this question we must remember that freedom is essential to honest inquiry, and that freedom is not compatible with an official position. We must also remember that when the State undertakes any duty, private persons are encouraged to think that they are absolved from exerting themselves. Consider what might be done to advance the knowledge and welfare of mankind by voluntary effort. If our rich men were really interested in religion, science, philanthropy—if they held their wealth and their business ability in trust for the community—they might provide for all these social purposes far more adequately than the State can hope to do. For the State can only obtain money by compulsion ; and it is at least questionable whether government should take so many pence in the pound out of many small incomes, in order to promote inquiries from which the owners of the said incomes may never derive any benefit.

Poor Relief.

The State leaves every subject free to make a living in his own way ; if he fails, the State is not responsible. At the same time, the State has to recognise that the imperfection of its own laws is one of the causes of poverty, and it admits that relief should be given where it is necessary to prevent starvation. This relief is given on grounds of expediency, and not as a right. If relief were a right, any citizen might claim and receive it; but, as things now stand, the man who accepts relief ceases to be a citizen; he must submit to be dealt with at the discretion of the authorities, and even to be confined in a workhouse if they think fit. This is a stern rule, but a very beneficent one. Nothing tends more directly to the degradation of the poor than an indulgent administration of the Poor Law.

There are some politicians who regard every case of poverty as a case for the interference of government; but the arguments by which they support this opinion are very lax. Thus they tell us that 'the State is the organised power of the community for good,' whereas in fact it is nothing of the sort. There are a thousand organised powers for good with which the State is not directly concerned. The State is an organised power set up for certain limited purposes; sometimes it is a power for good, sometimes for evil. Again, we are sometimes invited to promote 'generous' measures for relieving poverty; but the word 'generous,' when applied to legislation and administration, is wholly out of place. Suppose Parliament were to enact that all poor people should have certain comforts at the expense of the rates, where would be the generosity? Not in members of Parliament, for they are dealing with other people's money; not in the ratepayers, for no man pays rates except under compulsion.

Education.

The State leaves its subjects free to marry. If a

man marries and has children, he is responsible for their maintenance and education. But many parents have difficulty in meeting this responsibility; therefore large assistance is given to education from public funds. This assistance is not given as an absolute right. There are some who say that parents have a right to free schools, because they pay rates and taxes; but if this claim is admitted, I do not see what is to prevent parents from claiming free dinners for their children on the same ground.

Our system of public education rests on a very strong basis of expediency. It is an immense benefit to the community that every citizen should at least know how to read, and that those who desire knowledge should have facilities for obtaining it. So far from wishing the State to abandon its educational functions, we may find reasons for wishing to go further than we have yet gone. The State can make elementary education entirely free; can make our higher schools and colleges more accessible to all classes; can place technical information at the disposal of our artisans, and economical information at the disposal of the people generally.

But while we use the power of government in aid of education, we must do so cautiously, remembering that all coercive methods are attended with risk. Among the risks of State-aided education, these are worth considering.

First, we may impair the independence of parents and so do them an injury. A child gets for a penny that which costs the country sixpence. This may be good for the child and for society; but it is not an unmixed good for the parents. The benefit given savours of the old bad principle of rating in aid of wages. Again, if a middle-class man sends his son to college with the aid of a scholarship, that may be good for both, but it might in many cases be even better if the father made an effort and paid for his son.

State aid may do harm in another way, by imposing an official routine on the art of teaching. Education ought to vary with the needs and capacities of the pupil, but government education is the same for everybody. Hence the defects which are observed in our Board School system. Many weakly and ill-fed children are dragged with difficulty through studies which are easy enough for strong and well-fed children. And all children alike are made to devote the best part of their time to literary and grammatical knowledge, one result of which is, that the best pupils turn away even from skilled labour, and swell the crowd of competitors for clerkships.

Safety and Health.

During the present century the State has frequently been called in to protect its subjects against dangers to life and health. Hundreds of Acts of Parliament have been passed to regulate the management of factories, mines, and ships ; a little army of Inspectors has been set in motion to see that these Acts are duly observed ; the construction and drainage of houses have been placed under the supervision of public authorities ; and vaccination has been made compulsory.

Many of the results of this modern development of legislation have been satisfactory. The waste of infant life in our factories has been checked, and yet our industries have not been ruined, as the manufacturers prophesied they would be. Mines and ships are now managed with greater regard to the safety of the men employed. The mortality from small pox has been greatly reduced.

There is likely to be a great demand for sanitary and protective legislation in the immediate future, and we must be careful to see that the demand is not exaggerated. As soon as any malpractice is discovered, a cry goes up for another Act and another set of officials. Each of these demands must stand on its own merits, but there are some general considerations to be kept steadily in view.

First, the taste for inspectors is expensive. If every workshop and dwelling-house is placed under government supervision, a large sum must pass out of the pockets of the industrial classes in the shape of taxes, and into the pockets of officials in the shape of salaries.

Again, State inspection alone will not secure good sanitary conditions. Why is it that mines are often dangerous, and workmen's houses often unhealthy? Because landlords and employers think more of their profits than of the welfare of their tenants and workmen; and because the workmen are too apathetic, or too much at the mercy of employers to insist on having things set right. Legislation cannot touch the root of the evils complained of; it can only palliate their effects.

Industry and Trade.

Two centuries ago, no statesman doubted that governments were bound to encourage and direct the industries carried on by their subjects. Bounties were given to industries supposed to be profitable; prohibitive duties were laid on industries supposed to be unprofitable; every kind of business was placed under stringent rules, enforced by national and local authorities.

The greatest economists have always protested against these mistaken practices. They have taught us that if governments wish to encourage industry they had much better let it alone. People can find out for themselves what they can make and where they can sell it to advantage, what they want to use and where they can buy it to advantage. Every bounty, duty, or regulation implies a restriction on the free exchange of products, and no such restriction ought to be imposed, except for the purpose of preventing practices which are clearly injurious to the community. The end of industry is not production, but consumption, therefore products should not be prevented from passing freely into the hands of consumers.

The interest of the consumers (that is, of the general community) should always be placed first, the interest of the producers of any particular commodity must come second. Of course this doctrine is not always welcome to producers. If the workmen in any trade think they are injured by foreign competition, they are naturally unable to see why they should suffer in order that their neighbours may have more comforts. Therefore the labour vote in many countries is cast almost solid for Protection and State interference. It is not impossible that we may one day see a movement in favour of Protection among the labouring people of this country.

There is another mode in which modern governments

attempt to encourage industry. They place the credit of the State at the disposal of persons who are supposed to have some special claim to assistance. Money is raised on the credit of the State and lent to landlords who wish to drain their lands or to tenants who wish to purchase their holdings. Such loans are found useful in starting legislative experiments on a large scale; but they require to be carefully watched. Whether we are asked to lend to landlords or to peasants, the question arises, whether the security offered is good or bad. If it is good, the parties who require capital can obtain it on easy terms in the open market from private investors. If it is bad, the State is risking the money of the taxpayers (many of whom are far from well off) in promoting the interest of a favoured class. Nobody thinks it possible that the State can lend capital to everybody who desires to start in business. But if money is lent to drain land or to purchase a small property, why should it not be lent to a poor widow to start a small shop?

If the State lends money lavishly, it does a very questionable service to the objects of its 'generosity.' When landlords cannot raise money to drain their lands, the reason is that capitalists think the expenditure will not yield a good return. If this opinion is well founded, why encourage landlords to risk capital without return, when that same capital might yield a return, if employed in some other way? When a peasant cannot borrow money to buy his farm, the reason is that lenders know how difficult it is for a peasant owner to make his land pay. If this is so, why should politicians—who know far less about the matter than investors—insist on pretending that it is *not* difficult?

Summary.

The results arrived at in this and the foregoing chapter may be summarised as follows.

There are certain rough kinds of social work (national defence, repression of crime, etc.) which must be undertaken by the State, because they involve the use of force on a considerable scale.

There are other kinds of social work in which the State can give much assistance if it uses its force in a wise and timely manner, so as to check abuses and to introduce an element of system and discipline.

But in all its operations the State must be carefully watched, because all exercise of power brings with it temptations to official tyranny and waste of wealth. Our political ideal should be, not to place the individual at the mercy of the State, not to encourage the individual to look to the State for help, but rather to enable individuals, families, and private societies to work out their own honest purposes on their own responsibility.

The opinions of those who would restrict the State to the work of national defence, repression of crime, and enforcement of contract and property rights are expounded by Herbert Spencer: see his *Study of Sociology* and *The Man and the State*. For the progress of State Socialism in this country, see any recent report of the Trade Union Congress. The most comprehensive account of Socialism generally is E. de Laveleye's *Socialisme Contemporain*, of which there is an English translation.

CHAPTER XV.

THE STATE AND SOCIAL REFORM.

In the preceding chapters I have pointed out that the State works within limits, and that when statesmen pass beyond these limits they are likely to do as much harm as good. This is the doctrine of the greatest writers on social subjects. The jurists have taught us that 'law' always means 'force,' and we know that 'force is no remedy' for social disorders. The economists have shown us how industry is advanced by voluntary effort, and how it is often checked by the well-meant interference of legislators.

When politicians come into collision with jurists and economists, they seldom find it necessary to argue; they can always have recourse to rhetoric. They profess to be guided by the noblest sentiments (we know how unselfish party politicians are), and they affect to despise the 'narrow-minded' rules of the lawyer, and the 'cold-hearted' theories of the economist. So long as audiences are foolish enough to cheer this kind of nonsense, speakers will be found to utter it.

Some politicians go through life believing in an imaginary State, quite different from any actual State known to history. For an example, let us take Mr. Henry George. He has a profound contempt for all actual States. Monarchies and Republics are to him all alike—mere engines of oppression and spoliation. But Mr. Henry George wishes to make the State sole landlord--and why? Because he thinks that when the government comes to seize the land—that is, when he and his friends are in power—it will be an ideally pure and beneficent government, quite different from any actual government ever known.

State Socialism.

There are so many kinds of Socialism that a description which applies to all must of necessity be vague. We may say that a Socialist is distinguished from other politicians by the opinions which he professes concerning the causes of, and the remedies for, the great evil of poverty.

Socialists are, almost without exception, disciples of Rousseau. They assume that there was a time when all men had equal 'natural rights' in the earth and its produce, and that this system of equal rights was the cause of general happiness. They assume that private property had its origin in the desire of a few persons to deprive the many of their natural rights, and that the disorders of modern society are all due to the selfishness of the rich and the injustice of the laws which they have made.

In dealing with the facts of modern life, socialists love to dwell on the defects and failures of civilisation. They hold that things are going from bad to worse, 'the rich are becoming richer and the poor poorer.' They regard the labourer, not as an independent man, but as a helpless victim of selfish schemers; and they assure us that all attempts to reform society are useless, unless the labourer throws off the 'tyranny' of middle-class capitalists, and submits to the 'guidance' of certain middle-class politicians.

When they come to discuss the remedies for poverty, Socialists divide themselves into two sections. First, there are the Anarchists, who think that society is utterly bad, and must be destroyed so that some new form of human fellowship may arise 'naturally' on the ruins of the old. All that savours of authority must be annihilated—except, of course, the personal power of those who take the lead in the work of destruction. Bakunin, the Russian Nihilist, wished to abolish science itself, that the man of education might be in full sympathy with the people, and live together with them in a state of 'holy and wholesome ignorance.' These are not the views of sane men; it would be a waste of time to discuss them at any length.

The second party, the State Socialists, wish to strengthen existing authorities, and to employ them vigorously for the benefit of the poor. This is the aim of some despotic statesmen—Prince Bismarck, for example; it is also the aim of some authoritative democrats. Politicians of this school are seldom precise in their language. Mr. Chamberlain, for instance, who professes a kind of State Socialism, has told us that 'politics are the science of human happiness.' This definition is misleading, because it is far too wide. The art of politics has an important bearing on happiness; but its immediate subject is the just and economical conduct of public affairs. No government can make us happy; and considering how imperfectly government performs its special duties, we should be very foolish to entrust it with our happiness.

Most of the measures which compose the programme

of English State Socialists have already been incidentally noticed. It includes:—(1) Taxation: graduated so as to correct inequalities of fortune. (2) Loans of public money to persons too poor to borrow in the open market, and especially to persons who desire to purchase land in small quantities. (3) Enforcement of the duties attaching to property, and especially to large estates in land. (4) Local rates, levied on property, and administered by representative bodies, for the benefit of those who elect them. (5) Facilities for expropriating owners of land in the interest of their tenants or neighbours. It is not proposed, in this country, to expropriate owners of mills and factories, but it is sometimes suggested that government should own the mines and railways. (6) The State is to dictate the terms of contract between landlord and tenant, employer and employed; all agreements, except on the prescribed terms, to be absolutely void. It is not proposed to interfere with contracts between tradesman and customer, or between money-lender and borrower.

The proposals of State Socialism are perfectly legitimate. They do not involve any breach of the moral law; and those who resist them will do well to refrain from rhetorical appeals to the Eighth Commandment. But if they are not morally wrong, these proposals are open to grave objection on grounds of political justice and expediency. They all tend to increase the burden of taxation and officialism. They degrade our politics by teaching the people to exercise their electoral power with an eye to their own pecuniary benefit. You will also observe that the English State Socialists are singularly partial in their treatment of individuals and classes. Landlords' rights are to be freely cut down; but capitalists are to seek profits without any restriction. The peasant proprietor is to be favoured, but the small tradesman is to struggle on without assistance; and the small farmer is actually to be taxed to increase the number of competitors in his own already depressed industry.

State Socialism is not confined to any political party. It combines very readily with Toryism, and also with 'Tory democracy.' It is also found in alliance with Radicalism. There was a time when almost all Radicals disliked State intervention and favoured economy. But of late years they have been a prosperous party, and prosperity has altered their point of view. They are tempted now to say, 'If we can keep our own leaders in office, why, then *we* are the State; and we need have no pedantic scruples about extending our own powers.' The fact is that of all governments a popular well-meaning government requires to be most strictly watched and criticised.

What the State can do.

State Socialists usually endeavour to fix on their opponents the reproach of being mere critics, who object to every scheme of reform, and have no scheme of their own. There is some little truth in this charge; for the orthodox economists of our day have shown a certain want of readiness in developing the positive part of their doctrine. They have no difficulty in disposing of reasoners like Mr. Henry George;

but they are not so popular as Mr. George because they seem to have no gospel—no message of hope to poverty-stricken people.

It is, however, a great mistake to suppose that because economists take a cool estimate of facts and possibilities, therefore they take no interest in schemes of reform. They have a tolerably clear programme of their own, and this programme is well worth considering, though it may be less attractive at first sight than the sanguine promises of State Socialism. Let me indicate briefly some articles in the political creed of those who still believe in economic laws.

First, the State must recognise the limits of its own powers and must refrain from interfering with matters which it does not understand. We ought to place no confidence in party-leaders, unless they have the modesty to confess how little they can do to help us. And we must try to find leaders who will show us how to deal with poverty and other evils by voluntary effort.

The evils which afflict society are due partly to selfishness and partly to ignorance. Selfishness must be cured by moral agencies, and here the State is comparatively powerless. If a statesman wishes to correct the selfishness of one class, he usually effects his object by working on the self-interest of some other class.

In dealing with ignorance, the statesman is, or ought to be, more at home. The State possesses great facilities for collecting and disseminating information on questions of social interest, and these facilities ought to be actively developed. Let me enumerate some of the services which we may legitimately expect the State to perform for us.

1. Simplification of law. Our laws are pervaded by

a reasonable spirit, but they are voluminous in bulk, confused in arrangement, and obscure in style. They require to be re-arranged and expressed in plain English without needless involution and repetition. This work will never be undertaken until the people insist on having it done. At present there is hardly any demand for simplification, and the efforts of popular legislators add every year to the volume and complexity of our laws.

2. Simplification of government. Officialism is the characteristic weakness of the modern State. Public business ought to be so conducted that the people may understand clearly what is going on; and the citizens ought to have every opportunity of acting for themselves, without the intervention of salaried officials. This was the notion on which our ancient system of local government was based; but the old structure of our liberties has almost disappeared under the centralising laws of modern times. We must endeavour to restore the independence of the local community, reserving to the State only those powers of inspection which are necessary to prevent abuses.

3. Better provision for enquiry into public questions. At present the State usually refuses to inquire until its hand is forced by agitation. There ought to be systematic provision for timely enquiry into any matter which seems likely to become the cause of political disputes. And when enquiries are made, the results ought not to remain buried in blue books, accessible only to the few; they should be summarised in popular form and circulated widely among the people concerned.

4. Systematic communication between legal and

voluntary social agencies. This is a theme on which much might be written; let me take only one illustration. Both legal and voluntary agencies are at work in relieving the poor. Immense harm is done by the indiscriminate action of Guardians on the one hand, and by the equally indiscriminate action of charitable individuals on the other. If the two would combine their information, they might effect a very useful division of labour. Persons reduced to poverty by innocent misfortune ought to receive voluntary aid, given in such a way and to such an amount as to enable them to recover an independent position. Persons reduced to poverty by misconduct or want of thrift should be handed over to the Poor Law.

These reforms are not quite so ambitious as the schemes of the State Socialist. But they are possible; they contain no element of strife or disturbance; and they afford scope for all the energy and skill we can bring to bear on them.

Conclusion.

In all ages of the world there have been two schools of popular politics.

The doctrine of one school may be summed up in two maxims: *Give the State as little as you can*, and *Get as much out of the State as you can.*

The doctrine of the other and sounder school is precisely to the opposite effect. We ought to give the State as much as we can, bearing our share of common burdens willingly, and taking our full share of service. We ought to depend on the State as little as we can. The lumbering machine of Government is already overweighted; let us co-operate to reduce and not to increase the load.

INDEX.

Abstract politics, 42.
American democracy, 31.
Anarchists, 153.
Aristocracy, its origin, 12; its principle, 37.
Armies, national, 135.
Athens, type of Greek City, 16.
Authority based on religion, 20.

Bakunin, a Nihilist, 153.
Ballot Act, 62.
Bismarck, a Socialist, 153.

Candidates, choice of, 60; and the Caucus, ib.
Capital, nature of, 94.
Catholic theology, 20.
Centralisation, 53.
Chamberlain and Socialism, 153.
Church of Christ, origin, 19; political position, 141.
Civilisation, beginning of, 15.
Clans and chiefs, 12.
Classes of society, 127; the middle class, 25.
Competition, 98.
Conservative party, 80.
Constitution, 43.
Constitutional monarchy, 36.
Consumers considered first, 148.
Consumption of wealth, 92.
Cost defined, 96.
Crime, repression of, 138.
Cromwell and toleration, 26.
Custom and law, 9.

Demand and Supply, 100.
Democracy, its origin, 12; advance of, 31; principle of, 40.
Despotic monarchy, 35.
Diplomacy and popular government, 137.

Economists, their doctrine, 28; abused by politicians, 151.

Education and the State, 145.
Egypt, the ancient kingdom, 15.
Election laws, 54.
Equality an ideal, 73.
Exchange described, 93.
Executive government, 44.

Family, history of, 11.
Foreign affairs, 137.
Fraternity an ideal, 74.
Freedom defined, 68; free trade, 84, 147; freedom of contract, 114.

Generosity and the ratepayers, 144.
George, Henry, 151.
God and nature, 7; and monarchy, 35; and property in land, 104; and the law of population, 109.
Graduated taxation, 131.
Greek politics, 15.

Happiness an ideal, 75; and politics, 153.
Health and the State, 146.
Humanitarian philosophy, 26.

Ideals, 65.
Industry, modern, 28; encouraged by the State, 147.
Inequality, origin of, 126.
Interest, to whom paid, 118.

Jews, their customs, 9.
Judges should be independent, 48.
Justice, nature and kinds of, 68; criminal and civil, 138.

Labourers and the franchise, 56; labourer not always producer, 123.

INDEX

Land, common property in, 13; private property in, 103.
Legislation, 48; and justice, 69.
Liberal party, 82.
Liberty defined, 66.
Liverpool, Lord, 84.
Loans of public money, 149.
Local government, 52.

Machiavelli on politics, 24.
Malthus on population, 109.
Military service, 135.
Modern society, 22.

Napoleon, 27.
Nature and God, 7; and law, 18, natural rights, 72.

Officials, 45.
Order as an ideal, 65.
Origin of society, 5.

Parliament, 48; members not paid, 52.
Parties, 78.
People, the, not always right, 28, 32; 'will of the people,' 41.
Political economy, 90; does not teach selfishness, 110; not adverse to reform, 156.
Poverty and progress, 30; remedies for, 143, 158.
Primitive society, 9.
Production defined, 92; who are producers, 123.
Profit defined, 96; how distributed, 123.
Progress described, 32.
Property, its origin, 13; in land, 111; why protected by law, 111; diffusion of, 129.
Protection, 84.
Protestantism, 22.

Radical party, 84; and Socialism, 155.

Reformation and Renaissance, 22.
Rent defined, 106; how distributed, 118.
Republicanism, 36.
Revolution in France, 27; revolution and reform, 128.
Rights defined, 34; rights of man, 71.
Robespierre on the people, 27.
Roman law, 18; Holy Roman Empire, 20.
Rousseau and humanitarian theories, 6, 26, 152.

Salaries and fees, 119.
Science and the State, 142.
Secular politics, 24.
Self-interest a fact, 110.
Smith, Adam, 28.
Social contract, 5.
Socialism, 152.
Speculation described, 102.
State defined, 34; its functions, 134; its limits, 141.
Supply and demand, 100.

Three Estates, 49.
Toleration, its history, 23; its consequences, 141.
Tory democracy, 85, 155.
Tory party, 79.

Utilitarians, 75.
Utility defined, 91.

Value defined, 96.
Voluntary effort, 156.

Wages, how fixed, 120.
War a necessary evil, 135.
Wealth defined, 92.
Whig party, 81.
Will, right to make, 130.

THE END.

www.ingramcontent.com/pod-product-compliance
Lightning Source LLC
Chambersburg PA
CBHW030302170426
43202CB00009B/841